A BRAND-NEW YEAR—
A PROMISING NEW START

With expert readings and forecasts, you can chart a course to romance, adventure, good health, or career opportunities while gaining valuable insight into yourself and others. Offering a daily outlook for 18 full months, this fascinating guide shows you:

- The important dates in your life
- What to expect from an astrological reading
- How the stars can help you stay healthy and fit
  And more!

Let this sound advice guide you through a year of heavenly possibilities—for today and for every day of 2014!

SYDNEY OMARR'S® DAY-BY-DAY
ASTROLOGICAL GUIDE FOR

ARIES—March 21–April 19
TAURUS—April 20–May 20
GEMINI—May 21–June 20
CANCER—June 21–July 22
LEO—July 23–August 22
VIRGO—August 23–September 22
LIBRA—September 23–October 22
SCORPIO—October 23–November 21
SAGITTARIUS—November 22–December 21
CAPRICORN—December 22–January 19
AQUARIUS—January 20–February 18
PISCES—February 19–March 20

IN 2014

SYDNEY OMARR'S®

DAY-BY-DAY ASTROLOGICAL GUIDE FOR

CAPRICORN

DECEMBER 22–JANUARY 19

2014

by Trish MacGregor
with Rob MacGregor

A SIGNET BOOK

SIGNET
Published by the Penguin Group
Penguin Group (USA) Inc., 375 Hudson Street,
New York, New York 10014, USA

USA / Canada / UK / Ireland / Australia / New Zealand / India / South Africa / China

Penguin Books Ltd., Registered Offices: 80 Strand, London WC2R 0RL, England
For more information about the Penguin Group visit penguin.com.

First published by Signet, an imprint of New American Library,
a division of Penguin Group (USA) Inc.

First Printing, June 2013

Sydney Omarr's is a registered trademark of Writers House, LLC.

Sydney Omarr® is syndicated worldwide by Los Angeles Times Syndicate.

 REGISTERED TRADEMARK — MARCA REGISTRADA

ISBN 978-0-451-41395-6

Printed in the United States of America
10 9 8 7 6 5 4 3 2 1

ALWAYS LEARNING   PEARSON

CONTENTS

CHAPTER 1

The New You

We branded 2012 the year of the paradigm shift, and since the world didn't end, 2013 became the year of transformation. Now here you are at the doorstep of 2014, and the person who steps through is the new you!

And who is this new you likely to be? For some clues, let's take a look at the transits of the outer planets this year. These planets exert the most influence over our daily lives because they take so long to move through a single sign. Pluto, for instance, entered Capricorn in 2008 and won't leave until early 2024. Neptune, which takes about fourteen years to move through a sign, entered Pisces in early February 2012 and will be there until late January 2026. Uranus entered Aries in March 2011 and leaves that sign in March 2019. So just these three planets exert a powerful influence over a number of years.

The next two planets that influence us over a period of time are Saturn, which takes two and a half years to transit a sign, and Jupiter, which usually takes about a year. Each of these planets is covered extensively in various parts of the book, and each one has its role in the formation of the new you in 2014.

In the next chapter we talk about what each of the planets represents, what signs they rule, and just about anything else you could ever want to know about them astrologically. In a later chapter historical perspectives are provided on the three slowest-moving planets. But this chapter let's take an in-depth look at the planet Uranus and how its energies will help define the new you.

Uranus

This planet symbolizes revolution, genius, rebellion, earthquakes, sudden, unexpected events and change, our individuality, inventions and discoveries, electricity, radio, TV, electronics, lightning. You get the idea. Its energy isn't the least bit subtle. It sweeps into our lives, stirs up mass movements, and knocks down the old to make way for the new.

On March 11, 2011, the day that Uranus entered Aries, there was a 9.0 earthquake near the east coast of Honshu, Japan. The quake triggered a twenty-three-foot tsunami that hammered Japan's coast and caused an explosion at the Fukushima nuclear plant and the subsequent worst nuclear disaster since Chernobyl twenty-five years ago.

Any country would be devastated by just one of these events. But to have all three within twenty-four hours resulted in some staggering statistics. According to an earthquake report issued by http://earthquake-report.com, about twenty thousand people are either dead or missing; more than a million buildings were destroyed, eighty thousand residents were evacuated from a twelve-mile radius around the plant, and the economic losses range from between $100 to $500 billion, most of it created within seventy minutes.

As of late 2011 the evacuees have still not been permitted to go home, and the authorities are still cooling down the plant. The environmental ministry in Japan says an area of 930 square mi is affected.

All of these events are right in line with the archetypal energy of Uranus transiting Aries, the warrior.

Other facets of this transit are revolution and rebellion. First there were the uprisings in the Arab world in late 2010 that swept three leaders out of power—the heads of Tunisia, Egypt, and Libya. Then in September 2011 came a grassroots protest: Occupy Wall Street. On September 17 about two thousand people congregated in downtown Manhattan and marched up Broadway. En route they stopped at Zuccotti Park and more than a hundred of the protesters stayed the night and set up an encampment.

The mainstream media ignored the protest at first. Then Keith Olbermann, on Current TV, started covering it, and suddenly so did everyone else. From the Occupy Web site: ". . . we kicked off a protest against bank bailouts, corporate greed, and the unchecked power of Wall Street in Washington." The movement rapidly gained global support, and by its one-month anniversary had spread to eighty-two countries.

It takes eighty-four years for Uranus to move through the zodiac. So let's take a trip down memory lane to the last time Uranus transited the sign of Aries. In mid-January 1928 Uranus entered Aries and remained there until late March 1935. Here are some of the events that occurred during this period:

- First air-conditioned office opens in the U.S. in San Antonio
- Scotch tape first marketed by 3M company
- First trans-Atlantic TV image received
- Amelia Earhart first woman to fly the Atlantic — as a passenger
- Alexander Fleming discovers penicillin
- Yo-yo introduced
- First regularly scheduled TV is broadcast three nights a week
- German airship *Graf Zeppelin* begins a round-the-world flight
- Stock market crash
- Salvador Dali's first one-man show
- Bingo invented
- Planet Pluto named
- Hostess Twinkies invented
- N.Y. Yankee Babe Ruth hits three consecutive homers
- First nudist colony opens
- First radar detection of planes
- *N.Y. World* reports disappearance of supreme court justice Joseph Crater
- N.Y.C. College offers first course in radio advertising
- A bloodless coup d'état in Brazil
- First *Dracula* movie released
- Empire State Building opens in N.Y.C.
- Al Capone is indicted on 5,000 counts of prohibition and perjury

- Babe Ruth hits his 600th home run
- Alka Seltzer goes on sale
- Jane Addams—first U.S. woman named corecipient of Nobel Peace Prize
- Martial law is declared in Honduras to stop revolt by banana workers fired by United Fruit
- El Salvador army kills four thousand protesting farmers
- First patent issued for a tree, to James Markham for a peach tree
- Amelia Earhart is first woman to fly solo across the Atlantic
- Yellow fever vaccine for humans announced
- U.S. federal gas tax enacted
- Earthquake kills seventy thousand in Kansu, China
- Hitler proclaims end of Marxism
- Bank holidays declared in six states to prevent run on banks
- F.D.R. inaugurated as thirty-second pres, pledges to pull U.S. out of Depression and says, "We have nothing to fear but fear itself."
- F.D.R. proclaims ten-day bank holiday
- Dachau, first concentration camp, completed
- First flight over Mount Everest
- Nazis stage public book burnings in Germany
- Loch Ness Monster is first reported
- German Secret State Police (Gestapo) established
- In London five hundred thousand march against anti-Semitism
- Alcatraz officially becomes a federal prison
- *Flash Gordon* comic strip debuts

- F.D.R. signs Home Owners Loan Act
- First Sugar Bowl and first Orange Bowl
- First canned beer is sold
- Monopoly is invented
- First Penguin book is published
- Four hundred thousand demonstrators against fascism in Madrid
- *Billboard* magazine publishes its first music Hit Parade
- The first stock car race is held in Daytona Beach, Florida
- *Gone With the Wind* by Margaret Mitchell is published
- Spanish Civil War begins; General Francisco Franco leads uprising
- King Edward VIII abdicates throne to marry Mrs. Wallis Simpson

This list represents just a small sampling of the thousands of events that occurred during Uranus' last transit of Aries. But as you read through this list you undoubtedly see a pattern—war, rebellion, uprisings, numerous discoveries and many "firsts," the rise of Hitler and Nazi Germany, natural disasters like earthquakes, the completion of engineering marvels like the Empire State Building and Hoover Dam, the precipitous drop of the stock market and the depression that followed.

Aries is not only the sign of the warrior, but of the entrepreneur, the trailblazer, the one who is so independent and forward thinking that he marches to a different drummer. Aries is fearless, a risk-taker, and like the *Star Trek* motto, goes where no man (or woman) has gone before. So when you combine Aries with the planet that symbolizes all the traits mentioned earlier, you have an intriguing MO for the emergence of the new you.

The new you will be emerging into a new planetary environment, so let's start there.

Innovations

Book publishing. Once the dust settles, the book publishing industry and retail bookstores in general will be vastly changed from the way they have existed for years. The emergence of the eBook, the Kindle, Nook, and other electronic reading devices is, as of this writing in early 2012, creating chaos. With the bankruptcy of Borders Books, Barnes & Noble is the only game left in town, the largest book retailer in the U.S., and they don't stock every book that is published. So what happens to a book when Barnes & Noble doesn't carry it? That depends.

If the book is an eBook that sells for a fraction of the price of a hardback book—$9.99 versus, say, $25 or $30—perhaps the lack of hardcover sales are compensated for because more people can afford to buy an eBook than a hardcover. A young woman in Minnesota wrote a romance novel that was rejected by major publishers, so she self-published the novel as an eBook, sold it for $2.99, and sold millions of copies. Within a year she paid a million cash for her first home.

So what might we expect this year? Perhaps the publishing and bookstore industry are learning that life is interconnected. Ebooks, after all, save trees. Saving trees helps the environment. Helping the environment aids the planet. So perhaps by the time this transit is finished ebooks will be the norm, and only libraries will carry print books.

Another possible repercussion is that more authors will self-publish in ebooks. With the advent of blogs and online software that makes building a Web site easier than a few years ago, there may come a time when authors charge for access to their blogs, where entire novels and books are written.

More social media. MySpace, Facebook, Twitter, LinkedIn, Google Friends ... before Uranus leaves Aries, expect more social media to surface. Uranus rules the Internet, so the Internet itself may evolve and change in important ways before the end of this transit.

Medical breakthroughs. During Uranus' last transit of Aries, the medical breakthroughs were significant: treatment for yellow fever, development of penicillin, anesthesia, insulin shock therapy, vitamin B3, and protonsil, the first sulphur drug, which was used to treat infections caused by streptococcus. So this time around we can expect other types of breakthroughs in medicine, health, and pharmacology. A cure for AIDS? Cancer? Heart disease?

Rebellion/revolution. More planetary changes are likely, and so is continued rebellion by the 99 percent. The us-versus-them mentality has brought about a wider gap between rich and poor, with the middle class fading rapidly. Groups of urban survivalists have sprung up, some of them extremists.

The U.S., with the most powerful military in the world (which also eats up the largest chunk of the federal budget), continues to police the rest of the planet, while pushing the needs of its own citizens into a dark hole labeled *later*.

The contentiousness of the political divide in the U.S. was glaringly obvious in the health care debate that raged in early 2011 and later that year in the debt crisis debates. These trends, unfortunately, may get worse before Uranus leaves Aries.

However, if we remember that Uranus' job is to shake up the status quo so that new paradigms, new ways of doing things, can be born, then we could see the birth of new political parties that emphasize peace over war. Perhaps we'll see a complete withdrawal of U.S. troops from the Mideast.

Politics. The warrior archetype is certainly prevalent these days in politics. As a new paradigm is being birthed, the old paradigm isn't dying an easy death.

The meltdown in 2008 resulted in massive bailouts to banks, the collapse of institutions, and billions of stimulus dollars poured into the economy. It was the Obama administration's equivalent of F.D.R.'s New Deal, passed during his first term in response to the Great Depression. During this period Social Security was implemented.

As Uranus continues its transit through Aries, we may see the implementation of new social or economic programs that aid people rather than banks and corporations. It's doubtful we'll see any true universal health coverage, at least not if the past is any indication. But *if* a visionary was swept into the White House in 2016, *if* the corporate greed has been overturned, *if* Wall Street is regulated and the entire banking system overhauled, then maybe. But it's a lot of *if*s.

Discoveries. Numerous discoveries and inventions came about during Uranus's last pass through Aries. This transit could produce the twenty-first–century equivalents in technology, television, the Internet, health and medicine, engineering, movies, earthquake detection, music, ebooks, alternative fuels.

World records. During Uranus' last transit of Aries many "firsts" occurred, and world records were set. This time around we could see more of the same—in space flight, cars that run on alternative fuels, high-speed trains, athletics, even the ways our homes and office buildings are powered. The world may go green more quickly than we can imagine.

With Uranus, we either embrace change—or it's forced upon us. So let's take a look at how each of us can embrace the change Uranus is ushering into our personal lives.

Aries ♈

Cardinal Fire Sign

The new you is likely to be an improved version of the old you. The things you disliked about yourself a few years ago will fall away. Maybe a belief system you clung to a few years back was no longer serving your best interests and has now shattered, and you're casting about for new beliefs, new ways of being. Or perhaps a significant relationship has fallen apart. Or you lost your job. In whatever area your life was sterile and routine, Uranus has shaken things up.

As an Aries, you're probably well aware of where your life is stale and routine and do your best to turn it around. That means you're ahead of the game, and the Uranus transit through your sign will be exciting. But in the event you're the rare Aries who doesn't mind routine, this transit will be jarring, and the new you will emerge from the shock. Uranus has been in Aries for about three years now, so you should have a fairly clear idea how the transit is affecting you.

The best way for you to navigate this transit is to do what you do naturally: maintain a sense of adventure about life; be passionate in all that you undertake; keep your steady focus, don't hesitate to explore. In addition treat others the way you like to be treated. In love relationships strive to be more cooperative, to see things the way your partner does. In your career, with your creative work, complete what you start.

Unusual ideas and idiosyncratic individuals are part of this transit package. You won't be bored, but be careful that life doesn't become just one adrenaline high after the other. Welcome change, embrace it, even if it's thrust on you.

Taurus ♉

Fixed Earth Sign

Unless you have some planets in fire signs, you probably won't like this transit very much. It jars your grounded, Taurean sensibilities. However, because you're the most stubborn, resilient, and resolute sign in the zodiac, you come through it intact, with a new you to show to the world.

The new you in 2014 may be less stubborn, for one thing. The Uranus transit, after all, occurs in your solar twelfth house, so a lot of *stuff* is being stirred up in your unconscious. You may discover power you have disowned over the years and take it back. Or you may discover your dreams are filled with insights and information that aid you. Ideas that come to you during this transit are likely to be unusual, and it will be up to that grounded side of your personality to translate them into something useful.

As a fixed earth sign, you like things in your life to be orderly, practical, even predictable. You're slow to change your opinions and beliefs. *Stability* is your middle name. Since this transit occurs in your solar twelfth house, Uranus shakes up your world from the inside out. Your greatest strength during this period is to tackle one issue at a time and deal with it the way you do everything else in your life—carefully, thoroughly, meticulously.

The new you who emerges this year is the Taurus who has tackled these issues and reclaimed personal power and is ready to embrace everything that comes your way.

Gemini ♊
Mutable Air Sign

The new you who emerges in 2014 is likely to be more focused, ready to implement all the unusual ideas that are flowing through you. The way you implement these ideas, of course, is through your communication skills and by using your flexibility to quickly adapt to new situations.

Uranus forms a beneficial angle to your sun during

this transit, which enhances your innate abilities and attracts unusual people, excitement, and abrupt, positive change. It occurs in your solar eleventh house of friends, wishes, and dreams. The new you is apt to be more involved in a group—a theater group, writing, bridge, esoteric—that supports your interests and passions. In some way this group helps you to achieve your wishes and dreams.

New opportunities should surface for self-expression. If you've always had a secret yearning to write a novel or screenplay, for example, this transit helps you to do it. If you're an amateur photographer, you may have an opportunity to become a professional. The transit will free you from limiting circumstances—a relationship that no longer works, a job that has grown stale and predictable, a career that no longer feels right. Your comfortable ruts will become history.

Cancer ♋
Cardinal Water Sign

In 2014 the new you is a career-oriented individual. The Uranus transit through Aries forms a challenging angle to your sun and occurs in your tenth house of career, so you've probably experienced or are experiencing radical, abrupt professional changes. Your job, for example, could be outsourced. Or you get a new boss whom you don't like. Or you have to take a cut in pay. Whatever the curve ball that Uranus in Aries throws your way, Cancer, regard it as an opportunity, and watch the new you begin to take shape.

The new you will be able to draw steadily upon the

vast reservoir of your intuition, will gain immeasurably from insights and information gleaned from your dreams, and will be readily able to put these insights to work.

The lens through which you see the world is personal, subjective, emotional. Your nurturing and intuitive abilities are your greatest strengths and will serve the new you even better than they served the former you! You eagerly seek out the new and different and embrace change.

Leo ♌

Fixed Fire Sign

The new you who emerges from this transit will have vastly improved skills and talents and less ego. Uranus forms a beneficial angle to your sun during this transit and bolsters all the qualities for which you're known and loved—your warmth, compassion, flair for drama, and ability to make friends with just about anyone.

The sudden, exciting changes that are brought about prompt you to try new forms of self-expression. Your creative drive soars. The stimulating people you encounter during this transit, individuals who may be geniuses in their fields, may prove helpful to you in some way. There could be romance and love with this transit too, Leo. So many intriguing individuals are entering your life now that you'll have your pick!

The new you may undertake a spiritual quest of some kind and travel abroad in search of esoteric knowledge. Or you may go to college, grad school, or law school. You will make time to keep yourself fit and healthy through a regular fitness regimen.

Virgo ♍

Mutable Earth Sign

This transit forms a challenging angle to your sun sign and is shaking up those areas that have become routine in your life. The new you who emerges this year will still be a perfectionist who is precise and detailed oriented, but no longer to the point of obsession.

The transit occurs in your solar eighth house—shared resources. Since the eighth house represents joint resources, your partner's income may rise or fall suddenly or unexpectedly. You could inherit money. It's an excellent time to get out of debt. In fact, debt may be another limitation that you find intolerable. The new you will probably be more frugal, paying for things in cash.

Any new romance that comes your way could be highly sexual and have a deeply intuitive component to it.

Libra ♎

Cardinal Air Sign

The new you who emerges in 2014 will still possess all the wonderful qualities that make you the person so many people love. You will still be able to put yourself in someone else's shoes and see the world through the eyes of another. But you aren't as likely to bend over backward to please other people, and finding peace and harmony won't be as difficult as it may have been in the past.

The new you will reach out to people more readily. The social grace with which you do this will enable you to win over the opposition every time. This transit occurs in your solar seventh house of partnerships. Both romantic and business partnerships could be challenged during this transit, but you ride the tide, whatever it is, and learn from the experiences. When sudden, unexpected events bring about the beginning and end of partnerships, you stand up for who you are and what you really believe, and in doing so you break free of restrictions that have become unbearable.

This transit may seem harsh at times. It appears that stuff is happening *to* you, that the universe is ganging up against you. But what's actually happening is that energies you have repressed over the years are now scrambling for release. Any relationship that ends under this transit—through death or otherwise—does so because it has served its purpose. Relationships that begin during this transit are apt to be exciting, different in some way, and stimulating mentally, emotionally, and spiritually.

Go with the flow, Libra. That's the new you.

Scorpio ♏

Fixed Water Sign

The new you who emerges in 2014 is influenced by several factors—Uranus in Aries, certainly, but also by

Saturn transiting your sign, something we'll talk about in a later chapter. This new you will be more intuitive and less stubborn and perhaps less secretive as well. You will continue to delve deeply for answers, but in a less obsessive way. You won't be doing it with a feeling that it must be done immediately. Tomorrow or next week will work fine too.

This transit is about freedom—from restrictions and limitations in any area of your life that prevent you from evolving creatively, spiritually, or emotionally. As a fixed water sign, you probably don't like change any more than your fixed-sign brothers—Taurus, Leo, and Aquarius. But change you must. It's easier if you can learn to embrace change rather than resist it so that change isn't thrust on you, and that's what the new you achieves!

Since this transit occurs in your solar sixth house, the area most likely to be impacted is your daily work routine and health. The possible scenarios depend on how rigid, routine, or boring your daily work is; whether you stick to this work primarily because it's comfortable; and whether or not you enjoy what you're doing. The health aspect depends on how well you take care of yourself and your beliefs about health. In other words, if you believe that people get colds every winter, you probably will get a cold every winter. So take inventory of your beliefs, Scorpio. The new, emerging you has a clear handle on his or her beliefs.

Sagittarius ♐

Mutable Fire Sign

The new you who emerges from this Uranus transit, Sagittarius, is as exciting and adventurous as always, but with some important changes. You're now ready to actually be in a romantic partnership, to communicate honestly with your partner, to give for the joy of giving. It's likely that romantic relationships begin and end suddenly and your creativity is taking you in new directions. The new you is fine with whatever is happening. You eagerly embrace the changes in your life.

With Uranus in Aries forming a beneficial angle to your sun, you're able to become who you really are; it's much easier to reshape your personality. Your creative self-expression shines forth, and new venues for creativity open up. You may find yourself involved in creative projects that are totally different from anything you've done before, that prompt you to stretch your creativity in new ways.

If you're a Sadge who enjoys travel — and you probably are, many of your sign do — you'll be doing more of it during this transit. In fact, abundant foreign travel may be an intricate part of the new you.

Capricorn ♑

Cardinal Earth Sign

The new you who emerges in 2014 will be just as focused as you usually are, but with less of an obsessive edge. You're not obsessive the way a Scorpio is, for instance, but there can be an intensity about your focus that doesn't serve your best interests. Your ability to plow through any obstacle you encounter will enable you to break free of any limitations and restrictions that are either self-imposed or imposed on you by others. The new you will have better methods for doing this.

The transit occurs in your solar fourth house—your domestic environment—so let's take a look at some possible scenarios:

Your parents move in with you.

Your employer is relocating, and if you want to keep your job, you have to move too.

Your partner or spouse is laid off at work, and you have to sell your home and move to a smaller place.

Your parents get divorced, and you have to relocate.

The fourth house represents the foundation of your life, the most intimate and personal part of who you are. For most of us, changes in this area can be deeply unsettling. Any part of this area that has grown stale, rigid, or routine will be affected. But if your home life is vibrant and exciting, then it won't be impacted.

The new you will strive to be more flexible and will be better equipped to go with the flow emotionally, creatively, and spiritually.

Aquarius ♒

Fixed Air Sign

The new you who emerges this year will be edgier and more idiosyncratic, with more unusual ideas. The Uranus transit through Aries forms a beneficial angle to your sun and occurs in your solar third house, which represents communication, your conscious mind, neighborhood and neighbors, siblings, daily life, and travel. This area is where you're apt to experience all the excitement of this transit—and the place from which the new you emerges.

The new you is excited by the exploration of consciousness and how it molds and shapes our perceptions, and how, in fact, it may attract the kinds of experiences we have. During this transit your consciousness is expanding, leaping outward, seeking new ideas, and exploring different belief systems and lifestyles. You may move quite suddenly and unexpectedly, but it turns out to be beneficial for you. You may undertake creative projects that are outside your usual talents and abilities and discover a new facet of your personality. This period is all about trying the new and unexplored, adventures in consciousness and communication.

The new you knows it's the ideal time to start a blog, build a Web site, or write a novel or book and gets involved with community activities. Uranus, the planet that rules your sign, won't disappoint you during this transit.

Pisces ♓

Mutable Water Sign

The new you who emerges this year is just as imaginative and intuitive as always but less conflicted, so it's easier for you to make decisions. Like your mutable siblings—Gemini, Virgo, and Sagittarius—you don't have any problem with change. But because this transit occurs in a fire sign, Aries, your solar second house of finances, this is the area where the new you is likely to emerge.

The new you will insist on working in a profession or career that is in line with your deeper beliefs and ideals. The new you will follow intuitive leads, network with others of like mind, and strive to turn any challenge into a blessing. You'll understand that nothing is too wild to try, too *out there* to consider. The new you will understand the wisdom of financial prudence, will pay cash for everything, and probably cut up the credit cards too.

CHAPTER 2

Astrological Basics

On the day you were born, what was the weather like? If you were born at night, had the moon already risen? Was it full or the shape of a Cheshire cat's grin? Was the delivery ward quiet or bustling with activity? Unless your mom or dad has a very good memory, you'll probably never know the full details. But there's one thing you can know for sure: on the day you were born the sun was located in a particular zone of the zodiac, an imaginary 360-degree belt that circles the earth. The belt is divided into twelve 30-degree portions called signs.

If you were born between July 23 and August 22, the sun was passing through the sign of Leo, so we say that your sun sign is Leo. Each of the twelve signs has distinct attributes and characteristics. Leos, for instance, love being the center of attention. They're warm, compassionate people with a flair for the dramatic. Virgos, born between August 23 and September 22, are perfectionists with discriminating intellects and a genius for details. Capricorns, born between

December 22 and January 19, are the worker bees of the zodiac, serious minded, ambitious, industrious.

How Signs Are Classified

As you probably gathered from the first chapter, the twelve signs are categorized according to element and quality or modality. The first category, element, reads like a basic science lesson—fire, earth, air, and water—and describes the general physical characteristics of the signs.

Fire signs—Aries, Leo, Sagittarius—are warm, dynamic individuals who are always passionate about what they do.

Earth signs—Taurus, Virgo, Capricorn—are the builders of the zodiac, practical and efficient, grounded in everything they do.

Air signs—Gemini, Libra, Aquarius—are people who live mostly in the world of ideas. They are terrific communicators.

Water signs—Cancer, Scorpio, Pisces—live through their emotions, imaginations, and intuitions.

The second category describes how each sign operates in the physical world, how adaptable it is to circumstances:

Cardinal signs—Aries, Cancer, Libra, Capricorn—are initiators. These people are active, impatient, restless. They're great at starting things, but unless a project or a relationship holds their attention, they lose interest and may not finish what they start.

Fixed signs—Taurus, Leo, Scorpio, Aquarius—are deliberate, controlled, resolute. These individuals tend to move more slowly than cardinal signs, are often stubborn, and resist change. They seek roots and stability and are always in the game for the long haul. They aren't quitters.

Mutable signs — Gemini, Virgo, Sagittarius, Pisces — are adaptable. These people are flexible, changeable, communicative. They don't get locked into rigid patterns or belief systems.

TABLE 1 SUN SIGNS

Sign	Date	Element	Quality
Aries ♈	March 21–April 19	Fire	Cardinal
Taurus ♉	April 20–May 20	Earth	Fixed
Gemini ♊	May 21–June 21	Air	Mutable
Cancer ♋	June 22–July 22	Water	Cardinal
Leo ♌	July 23–August 22	Fire	Fixed
Virgo ♍	August 23–September 22	Earth	Mutable
Libra ♎	September 23–October 22	Air	Cardinal
Scorpio ♏	October 23–November 21	Water	Fixed
Sagittarius ♐	November 22–December 21	Fire	Mutable
Capricorn ♑	December 22–January 19	Earth	Cardinal
Aquarius ♒	January 20–February 18	Air	Fixed
Pisces ♓	February 19–March 20	Water	Mutable

The Planets

The planets in astrology are the players who make things happen. They're the characters in the story of your life. This story always begins with the sun, the giver of life.

Your sun sign describes your self-expression, your primal energy, the essence of who you are. It's the archetypal pattern of your Self. When you know another person's sun sign, you already have a great deal of information about that person. Let's say you're a Taurus who has just started dating a Gemini. How compatible are you?

On the surface, it wouldn't seem that you have much in common. Taurus is a fixed earth sign; Gemini is a mutable air sign. Taurus is persistent, stubborn, practical, a cultivator as opposed to an initiator. Gemini is a chameleon, a communicator, social, with a mind as quick as lightning. Taurus is ruled by Venus, which governs the arts, money, beauty, love, and romance, and Gemini is ruled by Mercury, which governs communication and travel. There doesn't seem to be much common ground. But before we write off this combination, let's look a little deeper.

Suppose the Taurus has Mercury in Gemini, and suppose the Gemini has Venus in Taurus? This would mean that the Taurus and Gemini each have their rulers in the other person's sign. They probably communicate well and enjoy travel and books (Mercury) and would see eye to eye on romance, art, and music (Venus). They might get along so well, in fact, that they collaborate on creative projects.

Each of us is also influenced by the other nine planets (the sun and moon are treated like planets in astrology) and the signs they were transiting when you were born. Suppose our Taurus and Gemini have the same moon sign? The moon rules our inner needs, emotions and intuition, and all that makes us feel secure within ourselves. Quite often compatible moon signs can overcome even the most glaring difference in sun signs because the two people share similar emotions.

In the sections on predictions your sun sign always takes center stage, and every prediction is based on the movement of the transiting planets in relation to your sun sign. Let's say you're a Sagittarius. Between November 16 and December 11 this year Venus will be transiting your sign. What's this mean for you? Well, since Venus rules—among other things—romance, you can expect your love life to pick up significantly during these weeks. Other people will find you attractive and be more open to your ideas, and you'll radiate a certain charisma. Your creative endeavors will move full steam ahead.

Table 2 provides an overview of the planets and the signs that they rule. Keep in mind that the moon is the swiftest-moving planet, changing signs about every two and a half days, and that Pluto is the snail of the zodiac, taking as long as thirty years to transit a single sign. Although the faster-moving planets—the moon, Mercury, Venus, and Mars—have an impact on our lives, it's the slow pokes—Uranus, Neptune, and Pluto—that bring about the most profound influence and change. Jupiter and Saturn fall between the others in terms of speed. This year Jupiter spends the first six months in Cancer, then enters Leo on July 16 and doesn't leave that sign until August 11, 2015.

In the section on predictions the most frequent references are to the transits of Mercury, Venus, and Mars and the movements of the transiting moon.

Now glance through Table 2. When a sign is in parentheses, it means the planet corules that sign. This assignation dates back to when we thought there were only seven planets in the solar system. But since there were still twelve signs, some of the planets had to do double duty!

TABLE 2 THE PLANETS

Planet	Rules	Attributes of Planet
Sun ☉	Leo	Self-expression, primal energy, creative ability, ego, individuality
Moon ☽	Cancer	Emotions, intuition, mother or wife, security
Mercury ☿	Gemini, Virgo	Intellect, mental acuity, communication, logic, reasoning, travel, contracts
Venus ♀	Taurus, Libra	Love, romance, beauty, artistic instincts, the arts, music, material and financial resources
Mars ♂	Aries (Scorpio)	Physical and sexual energy, aggression, drive
Jupiter ♃	Sagittarius (Pisces)	Luck, expansion, success, prosperity, growth, creativity, spiritual interests, higher education, law
Saturn ♄	Capricorn (Aquarius)	Laws of physical universe, discipline, responsibility, structure, karma, authority
Uranus ♅	Aquarius	Individuality, genius, eccentricity, originality, science, revolution

Planet	Rules	Attributes of Planet
Neptune ♆	Pisces	Visionary self, illusions, what's hidden, psychic ability, dissolution of ego boundaries, spiritual insights, dreams
Pluto ♀ ♇	Scorpio	The darker side, death, sex, regeneration, rebirth, profound and permanent change, transformation

Houses and Rising Signs

In the instant you drew your first breath, one of the signs of the zodiac was just passing over the eastern horizon. Astrologers refer to this as the rising sign or ascendant. It's what makes your horoscope unique. Think of your ascendant as the front door of your horoscope, the place where you enter into this life and begin your journey.

Your ascendant is based on the exact moment of your birth, and the other signs follow counterclockwise. If you have Taurus rising, for example, that is the cusp of your first house. The cusp of the second would be Gemini, of the third Cancer, and so on around the horoscope circle in a counterclockwise direction. Each house governs a particular area of life, which is outlined below.

The best way to find out your rising sign is to have your horoscope drawn up by an astrologer. For those of you with access to the Internet, though, there are several sites that provide free birth horoscopes: www

.astro.com and www.cafeastrology.com are two good ones.

In a horoscope the ascendant (cusp of the first house), IC (cusp of the fourth house), descendant (cusp of the seventh house) and MC (cusp of the tenth house) are considered to be the most critical angles. Any planets that fall close to these angles are extremely important in the overall astrological picture of who you are. By the same token, planets that fall in the first, fourth, seventh, and tenth houses are also considered to be important.

Now here's a rundown on what the houses mean.

Ascendant or Rising: The First of Four Important Critical Angles in a Horoscope

- How other people see you
- How you present yourself to the world
- Your physical appearance

First House: Personality

- Early childhood
- Your ego
- Your body type and how you feel about your body
- General physical health
- Defense mechanisms
- Your creative thrust

Second House: Personal Values

- How you earn and spend your money
- Your personal values
- Your material resources and assets
- Your attitudes and beliefs toward money
- Your possessions and your attitude toward those possessions
- Your self-worth
- Your attitudes about creativity

Third House: Communication and Learning

- Personal expression
- Intellect and mental attitudes and perceptions
- Siblings, neighbors, and relatives
- How you learn
- School until college
- Reading, writing, teaching
- Short trips (the grocery store versus Europe in seven days)
- Earth-bound transportation
- Creativity as a communication device

IC or Fourth House Cusp: The Second Critical Angle in a Horoscope

- Sign on IC describes the qualities and traits of your home during early childhood
- Describes roots of your creative abilities and talents

Fourth House: Your Roots

- Personal/domestic environment
- Your home
- Your attitudes toward family
- Early childhood conditioning
- Real estate
- Your nurturing parent

Some astrologers say this house belongs to Mom or her equivalent in your life, others say it belongs to Dad or his equivalent. It makes sense to us that it's Mom because the fourth house is ruled by the moon, which rules mothers. But in this day and age, when parental roles are in flux, the only hard and fast rule is that the fourth belongs to the parent who nurtures you most of the time.

- The conditions at the end of your life
- Early childhood support of your creativity and interests

Fifth House: Children and Creativity

- Kids, your firstborn in particular
- Love affairs, romance
- What you enjoy
- Creative ability
- Gambling and speculation
- Pets

Traditionally, pets belong in the sixth house. But that definition stems from the days when "pets" were chattel. These days we don't even refer to them as pets. They are animal companions who bring us pleasure.

Sixth House: Work and Responsibility

- Day-to-day working conditions and environment
- Competence and skills
- Your experience of employees and employers
- Duty to work, to employees
- Health and the daily maintenance of your health

Descendant/Seventh House Cusp: The Third Critical Angle in a Horoscope

- The sign on the house cusp describes the qualities sought in intimate or business relationships
- Describes qualities of creative partnerships

Seventh House: Partnerships and Marriage

- Marriage
- Marriage partner
- Significant others
- Business partnerships
- Close friends
- Open enemies
- Contracts

Eighth House: Transformation

- Sexuality as transformation
- Secrets

- Death, taxes, inheritances, insurance, mortgages and loans
- Resources shared with others
- Your partner's finances
- The occult (read: astrology, reincarnation, UFOs, everything weird and strange)
- Your hidden talents
- Psychology
- Life-threatening illnesses
- Your creative depths

Ninth House: Worldview

- Philosophy and religion
- The law, courts, judicial system
- Publishing
- Foreign travels and cultures
- College, graduate school
- Spiritual beliefs
- Travel abroad

MC or Cusp of Tenth House: The Fourth Critical Angle in a Horoscope

- Sign on cusp of MC describes qualities you seek in a profession
- Your public image
- Your creative and professional achievements

Tenth House: Profession and Career

- Public image as opposed to a job that merely pays the bills (sixth house)
- Your status and position in the world
- The authoritarian parent and authority in general
- People who hold power over you
- Your public life
- Your career/profession

Eleventh House: Ideals and Dreams

- Peer groups
- Social circles (your writers' group, your mother's bridge club)
- Your dreams and aspirations
- How you can realize your dreams

Twelfth House: Personal Unconscious

- Power you have disowned that must be claimed again
- Institutions—hospitals, prisons, nursing homes—and what is hidden
- What you must confront this time around, your karma, issues brought in from other lives
- Psychic gifts and abilities
- Healing talents
- What you give unconditionally

In the section on predictions you'll find references to transiting planets moving into certain houses. These houses are actually solar houses that are created by putting your sun sign on the ascendant. This technique is how most predictions are made for the general public rather than for specific individuals.

Lunations

Every year there are twelve new moons and twelve full moons, with some years having thirteen full moons. The extra full moon is called the Blue Moon. New moons are typically when we should begin new projects, set new goals, seek new opportunities. They're times for beginnings. They usher in new opportunities according to house and sign.

Two weeks after each new moon, there's a full moon. This is the time of harvest, fruition, when we reap what we've sown.

Whenever a new moon falls in your sign, take time to brainstorm what you would like to achieve during weeks and months until the full moon falls in your sign. These goals can be in any area of your life. Or you can simply take the time on each new moon to set up goals and strategies for what you would like to achieve or manifest during the next two weeks—until the full moon—or until the next new moon.

Here's a list of all the new moons and full moons during 2014. The asterisk beside any new-moon entry indicates a solar eclipse; the asterisk next to a full-moon entry indicates a lunar eclipse.

TABLE 3
LUNATIONS OF 2014

New Moons	Full Moons
January 1–Capricorn	January 15–Cancer
January 30–Aquarius	February 14–Leo
March 1–Pisces	March 16–Virgo
March 30–Aries	*April 15–Libra
April 29–Taurus*	May 14–Scorpio
May 28–Gemini	June 13–Sagittarius
June 27–Cancer	July 12–Capricorn
July 26–Leo	August 10–Aquarius
August 25–Virgo	September 8–Pisces
September 24–Libra	*October 8–Aries
October 23–Scorpio*	November 6–Taurus
November 22–Sagittarius	December 6–Gemini
December 21–Capricorn	

Every year there are two lunar and two solar eclipses, separated from one another by about two weeks. Lunar eclipses tend to deal with emotional issues, our internal world, and often bring an emotional issue to the surface related to the sign and house in which the eclipse falls. They can also result in news. Solar eclipses deal with events and often enable us to see something that has eluded us. They also symbolize beginnings and endings.

Read more about eclipses in the big picture for your sign for 2014. I also recommend Celeste Teal's excellent book, *Eclipses*.

Mercury Retrograde

Every year Mercury—the planet that symbolizes communication and travel—turns retrograde three times. During these periods our travel plans often go awry, communication breaks down, computers go berserk, cars or appliances develop problems. You get the idea. Things in our daily lives don't work as smoothly as we would like.

Here are some guidelines to follow for Mercury retrogrades:

Try not to travel. But if you have to, be flexible and think of it as an adventure. If you're stuck overnight in an airport in Houston or Atlanta, though, the adventure part of this could be a stretch.

Don't sign contracts—unless you don't mind revisiting them when Mercury is direct again.

Communicate as succinctly and clearly as possible.

Back up all computer files. Use an external hard drive and/or a flash drive. If you've had a computer crash, you already know how frustrating it can be to reconstruct your files.

Don't buy expensive electronics. Expensive anything.

Don't submit manuscripts, screenplays, pitch ideas, or launch new projects.

Revise, rewrite, rethink, review.

In the overview for each sign, check out the dates for this year's Mercury retrogrades and how these retrogrades are likely to impact you. Do the same for eclipses.

Other Retrogrades

Every planet except the sun and moon turns retrograde. So let's look at the retrogrades that will occur in 2014.

Venus: Retrograde in Capricorn from January 1 to January 31. This retro is continuation of one that began at the tail end of 2013. Venus retros can cause rough patches in your most intimate relationships. It can also bring about physical inconveniences and discomforts—your AC or heat goes out in the office, at home, or even in your car. Avoid buying luxury items during a Venus retro. That said, good deals can be found during a Venus retrograde. We once bought a car that we traded in a year later for the same price that we paid for it.

Mars: Retrograde in Libra from March 1 to May 19. Since Mars represents your sexuality, ambition, and physicality, best to check your natal chart to find out where you have Libra.

Jupiter: January 1 to March 6, retrograde in Cancer. This retro is a continuation from 2013. During this period your finances may be depressed, your luck factor isn't operating at full potential, and there could be setbacks or delays with publishing and educational ventures. Since the retro falls in Cancer, it's possible there are delays or setbacks at home too.

Saturn: March 2 to July 20. Retrograde in Scorpio. You discover which structures in your life need bolstering. Profits may be depressed.

Uranus: July 21 to December 21. Retrograde in Aries. Upheavals and changes occur, you feel unsettled, you may feel that your uniqueness is being squashed by a situation or relationship.

Neptune: June 9 to November 15. Retrograde in Pisces. Your creativity and ability to envision what you desire are limited in some way.

Pluto: April 14 to September 22. Retrograde in Capricorn. You may feel powerless or unmotivated in some area of your life.

CHAPTER 3

Love and Romance in 2014

Regardless of what kind of craziness is going on in the world around us, we still fall in love, commit to someone, get engaged or married. But our lives are certainly influenced by our environments, and in changing times we may become more independent or needier, our priorities may shift, or we may reach out for new relationships because we have outgrown the old ones. Or they may have outgrown us.

Let's start with your natal Venus. If you don't know what sign and house Venus was in when you were born, check http://www.astro.com/cgi/ade.cgi and enter your birth data. If you don't know the exact time of your birth, put in twelve noon so you can at least see what sign Venus was in when you were born.

The sign and house placement of your natal Venus tells you a great deal about your capacity for loving another and for being loved and your attitudes about love and romance. It also reveals how you approach your creativity, money, beauty, and females. If you're a Taurus or a Libra, Venus rules your sign, and if you have either of those signs rising, Venus rules your chart. It means the placement of Venus in your natal chart is particularly important.

In a man's chart the sign and house placement of Venus can indicate the kind of women to whom he's attracted. It can also reveal something about his relationship with his daughter, if he has one. In a woman's chart Venus indicates relationships with other women and with a daughter, if she has one.

So let's take a look at what your natal Venus means in terms of its sign and house placement:

Venus in the Signs

Venus in Aries

You take risks in romantic relationships. You tend to be passionate and impulsive and may be somewhat self-centered when it comes to romance and love. You're a terrific initiator when it comes to making money, but your money may go out as fast as it comes in. You're also adept at initiating creative projects, but if you lose interest along the way, you drop the project and move on to something new.

Venus in Taurus

Venus rules Taurus, so it's happy here and functions well. You're a sensuous individual, at times even lusty. You form deep emotional attachments in love and romance, and once you meet the right person are fully committed. You can be exceptionally stubborn about having things your way in a relationship. You attract money and prosperity, particularly if you work actively with your beliefs. Your creative expression is heightened by your sensuality. Once you start something, you're rarely a quitter!

Venus in Gemini

You have great charm and wit and can talk to anyone about anything. Your romantic relationships may not last long, and you may be involved with several people at once. You're not consciously fickle, but you simply get bored easily and move on. Two marriages are possible. On the creative front, you have so many interests and talents that it's sometimes difficult for you to choose what you would like to do most. Self-expression comes easily to you.

Venus in Cancer

You're a nurturing, compassionate individual. Home and marriage are important to you, and your family ties are strong. When you commit to a relationship, you commit completely. But until you're committed, there can be a tendency toward secret love affairs. You nurture your own creative abilities and skills with a resoluteness that others admire. You're not a quitter any more than Venus in Taurus is! You benefit through real estate and land and spend money freely on your home and family.

Venus in Leo

Like Venus in Aries, you have great passion and are ardent in your relationships. Your gregarious nature makes you the life of any party and attracts romantic interests easily and with hardly any effort on your part. In any romantic relationship, though, you like your partner to compliment you, notice you, court, and seduce you. You may have creative talent in the performing arts—theater, dance—or become publicly prominent.

Venus in Virgo

You have discriminating tastes in romantic relationships and may keep a mental list of qualities a partner must have. You're analytical about love—until the right person enters your life and sweeps you away. Then that mental list goes straight out the window. You can be self-critical in a relationship and also critical of your partner or about elements in the relationship. The quest of Venus in Virgo is to polish the diamond until it's the best there is. When it comes to artistic expression, you're a perfectionist, the kind of person who insists that all Ts are crossed. You're exceptionally good at any form of communication.

Venus in Libra

Venus rules this sign, so the planet is happy here, just as it is in Taurus. In romance and love you may have an idealized picture of how things are supposed to be and may bend over backward to make that idealized version happen. You seek harmony and peace in all your relationships—the very things that may elude you. Your artistic strengths are considerable and varied. There may be talent with writing, music, art, photography, or singing. You enjoy beauty in all its forms and don't hesitate to spend money on the things you love.

Venus in Scorpio

You have a passionate, sexual nature and are forever seeking the absolute bottom line in a relationship. When someone interests you, that person's pubic persona isn't enough for you. You dig deeper, scratching way beneath the surface, uncovering the individual's secrets and his or her hidden life. This propensity can lead to stormy relationships until you meet someone who erects strong boundaries. Your creativity springs from the deepest levels of your being and is often inspired. You might, for instance, be a pianist who can't read music and plays entirely by ear. Or you might be an artist who never took an art lesson in your life.

Venus in Sagittarius

Just like Venus in Aries and Leo, the other two fire signs, you love passionately. Your generous nature sometimes prompts you to wear your heart on your sleeve. You seek a partner who loves to travel as much as you do and who shares your love of animals and the arts. But when your personal freedom is threatened in some way, when a relationship makes you feel penned in, your passion cools quickly, and you immediately extricate yourself from the relationship. Creatively you seek the larger picture of whatever you're doing and leave the finer details to others.

Venus in Capricorn

Your capacity for love runs deep, but you are often restrained in how you express it. This restraint may be the result of a lack of trust in yourself or the other person, but it can also simply be one of your patterns, something that began when you were very young. Sexually however all the restraints and reserve fall away and your true passions burst forth. You strive to achieve financial and material assets and work hard to do so.

Venus in Aquarius

For you love and romance must start with an intellectual camaraderie, an exchange of ideas. You enjoy the company of idiosyncratic individuals, people out of the mainstream who have unusual ideas, occupations, or perceptions. You have many friends and among them may be a person who interests you romantically. In romantic relationships you need intellectual stimulation. Your financial habits could be erratic, or you may earn your living in an unusual way. Creatively you're a trendsetter.

Venus in Pisces

Your compassionate nature is practically legendary among people who know you. In love you're a true romantic, the kind of person who enjoys moonlit walks on beaches. It's this idealism, though, that sometimes gets you into trouble if the reality doesn't measure up. In a relationship your sensitivity to your partner's moods often borders on psychic. Romantic relationships and emotional attachments are necessary for your well-being.

Venus in the Houses

First house

You're a natural charmer, friendly, and probably physically attractive. You may have some unique talent that finds expression in art or music. You love literature and poetry and have a fondness for beautiful surroundings. This placement is usually fortunate—unless Venus is poorly aspected—and things generally come to you with ease. The closer Venus is to the ascendant—the rising—the more pronounced these qualities are.

Second house

Financial comfort, perhaps even wealth. You benefit financially from marriage and partnerships. You're probably an extravagant spender, but you can usually afford it, so it's not an issue. Your personal values are important to you, and you spend time and effort developing them.

Third house

You converse easily with people and are comfortable in your neighborhood or community. You're close to your siblings, other relatives, and neighbors and have excellent rapport with your immediate family. The love of your life may be someone you meet in your community or through relatives.

Fourth house

Your home and family are important to you and vital to your well-being. You seek harmony in your domestic environment and go to great lengths to maintain it. It's possible that you meet the love of your life early in life and then meet again later on when you're adults. You have a great rapport with your parents and gain financially through them. The closer Venus is to the cusp of the fourth house, the more pronounced these attributes will be.

Fifth house

For love, romance, children, and creative endeavors, this is where Venus is really at home. The fifth-house placement is great for happy love affairs, artistic projects, and anything creative. Your children may have unusual talents. You gain through romantic partners, children, and any sort of creative endeavor. Your undoing may be excessive pleasure!

Sixth house

Your daily work is a source of pleasure for you. You enjoy what you do, whatever it is, and probably have harmonious relationships with your coworkers. You're able to integrate your creativity into your daily work, and other people appreciate and admire your work.

This placement favors good health generally, but you should avoid excessive use of alcohol and drugs. In terms of romance you may work with the one you love!

Seventh house

Venus is happy here. It's likely that you'll have a happy marriage and profitable partnerships generally. You and your partner may work together in some capacity, perhaps moving toward a common goal—self-employment, for instance. You're a magnet for attracting what you need in partnerships and financial benefits.

Eighth house

You gain financially through marriage and partner-ships, inheritances, taxes, and contracts. You're lucky when it comes to other people's money and resources. You may have unusual and positive experiences with metaphysics. Love and romance with someone you knew in a past life are possible.

Ninth house

Romance and love may find you while you're travel-ing overseas. Music and art with spiritual themes in-trigue you, and you may have talent yourself in these areas. This placement of Venus favors involvement with publishing, spiritual groups, higher education, and foreign travel.

Tenth house

Talk about popularity! Writers, artists, entertainers, actors, novelists, reporters, and diplomats are all indicated by this placement. You're at ease in any kind of social venue, and other people are attracted to you and your ideas. Career matters and your professional life generally tend to unfold smoothly with little effort on your part. You may be "married" to your career or find love with someone who works in your profession. The closer Venus falls to the cusp of the tenth house, the more pronounced the qualities.

Eleventh house

Friendships and groups are important to you. They help you to achieve your wishes and dreams and share your interests in the arts, music, and books. You invest a lot of time and energy in your friendships, particularly with women, and could meet someone special through friends.

Twelfth house

Secret love affairs and romantic intrigues are indicated. You may work in solitude or behind the scenes in some sort of artistic profession. You enjoy mystery and adventure and actually enjoy the dramas of romantic intrigues.

Venus Transits and Retrogrades

Unless Venus is retrograde, as it is in 2014, a Venus transit lasts from three to four weeks. The times to watch for are when Venus returns to the place where it was when you were born and when Venus conjuncts your sun.

The first period is called a Venus return and is usually a genuinely enjoyable period. You have all the support you need or want from friends and partners. Everything that is promised in the natal placement of Venus is enhanced.

The second period is also terrific. It enhances all the qualities of your sun sign, bolsters your self-confidence, artistic inspirations, and ambitions and should do wonders for your love life.

In 2014 Venus begins the year retrograde in Capricorn and turns direct on January 31. These retrograde periods can be tough on your love life and your artistic expression. Or you may find yourself dealing with issues from the past in either of these areas. Another possibility with Venus retrograde is that your physical comfort may be compromised in some way. Perhaps the air conditioning or heat in your office building goes on the fritz, or maybe the defroster, heat, or AC in your car stops working.

This year, Venus transits Capricorn twice—at the beginning of the year and again briefly at the end. In between it moves through all the other signs as well. For specifics on how Venus transits affect your sign, read chapter 14.

CHAPTER 4

Finances in 2014

More than four years after the financial meltdown in 2008—when the "too big to fail" banks were bailed out, the housing market bottomed out, and unemployment burgeoned—the situation hasn't improved.

According to www.forecasts.org, unemployment by the spring of 2012 is supposed to be at 10.3 percent, and unless the economy turns around, that figure may be much higher by 2014. Despite the Obama administration's "homeowner bailout" programs, six million Americans are either behind on their mortgage payments or facing foreclosure, and millions more are underwater on their mortgages. An article in the *Las Vegas Sun* estimates that as of late 2011 American homeowners owe $700 billion to $800 billion more than their homes are actually worth.

A report in Huffington Post in October 2011 revealed half of borrowers with prime loans—those loans made to individuals with good credit and income—will likely end up underwater. A Fitch ratings report found that with home prices expected to drop in value by another 10 percent, at least half of prime borrowers will end up underwater. Complicating the situation, of course, are unemployment, underemployment, and the rising costs of goods.

How fast are those costs rising? Do your own test. What products do you use regularly? How much have their prices risen in the past year? A year ago our favorite coffee, a Cuban brand, used to sell for $2.59 a pound. The price has doubled. A dozen eggs that cost a buck a year ago are now twice that. A loaf of bread that used to cost a buck now costs three times that. You get the idea here, and you've no doubt noticed the rise in costs in your own life just for basics. When you include the prices of gasoline, electricity, tuition for college, and everything else, it's no wonder the middle class is shrinking.

The reality points to a pattern that has been prevalent throughout the twenty-first century—greed. Whether it's corporate or individual greed, there are no free rides. Banks lent to people who didn't have the income to meet mortgage payments and bundled good and bad mortgages together and sold them off. Borrowers used their homes as ATM machines. In a sense what is happening to the American economy is a reflection of what has happened to the U.S. economy overall: we are living beyond our means.

On the other hand, there are plenty of homeowners who weren't living beyond their means but whose lives changed dramatically when they were laid off or got sick, or their income was somehow diminished. You probably know people in your own community who have suffered in this way.

So what do all these depressing statistics means for you in 2014? A couple of things. If you've been hit badly by this economy, the first thing you should so is become politically active. It's not enough to vote in elections. Democracy is also about expressing your opinion. Occupy Wall Street started as a genuine grassroots movement and hit a nerve with the nation's young people. What started as a small protest on September 17, 2011, became a global movement within a month. That kind of activism is what helps to usher in a change in the status quo.

Take stock of your particular abilities and talents. Is there something you can do that would fill a niche in the market? Adversity, after all, can be an opportunity that prompts you to perceive your own skills in a different way and to see the market with new eyes.

What can you change about the way you live? Do you stash away a percentage of everything you make? Do you spend money as quickly as it comes in? Do you have a realistic budget? Are you in credit card debt? Do you live debt free? Depending on your financial situation, here are tips for each sign on how to maximize your potential this year; when the stars favor your finances—and when they don't.

But first take this inventory about your beliefs concerning money.

Belief Inventory

Here's a list of some commonly held negative beliefs about money. Check the ones to which you subscribe:

- Money is the root of all evil
- Money is nonspiritual

- The rich have major problems in their lives
- Money corrupts
- If you have too much money, you have to worry about losing it
- If you have too much money, it takes over your life.
- The wealthy don't have money problems, but they have a lot of other problems.

Many of these beliefs we've adopted from family and peers and have held on to them because they're comfortable, we believe they're true, or because we don't even realize we believe them! So if you're not satisfied with what you're earning, start monitoring how you think about money. Any time you find yourself thinking a negative thought about money, turn the thought around by thinking something more positive. Also, read Napoleon Hills' classic *Think and Grow Rich* and *Money and the Law of Attraction* by Esther and Jerry Hicks.

Now let's take a look at how you can maximize your earning potential in 2014.

Aries

There's a reason you're called the trailblazer, the entrepreneur. You see opportunities where others may not and figure out a way to turn those opportunities into money. You're the type who, in the midst of the Great Depression, might have launched your own business and filled a gap you recognized in the market. Adversity doesn't scare you; it becomes your booster rocket.

There are two excellent periods this year for finances. The first period falls between May 2 and 28, when Venus is in your sign. This period is excellent for earning additional money, sales, and asking for a raise. The second period, when Venus transits Taurus and your financial area, falls between May 28 and June 23. During this period you may be more prone toward saving rather than spending. But if you do feel the urge to spend, it may be for high-end items—art, jewelry. So if you succumb to the urge, be sure to pay cash!

Although we talk about Jupiter transits in a later chapter, this planet's transit through fellow fire sign Leo could be quite nice for your finances. That time frame: July 16, 2014, to August 11, 2015.

Excellent backup dates: September 13 to October 26, when Mars transits fellow fire sign Sagittarius.

Taurus

Many of you are artistic, good with money and investments, fashion, the culinary arts, photography, writing, music. In fact, you probably have numerous talents but because you tend to be somewhat reserved, other people don't know about them. Well, now is the time to let your true self shine, Taurus. And once you do, once you embrace all you are, then the opportunities begin to arrive, and you may have a chance to earn your living doing what you love.

An excellent time this year for maximizing your earning potential falls between May 28 and June 23, when Venus is in your sign. This period is one in which you feel extremely good about yourself and life in general, and that feeling bolsters your self-confidence. Others pick up on this, and suddenly, Taurus, you can do no wrong. You get hired for that job you want; you land a promotion or raise; you sell your novel.

The next period that could pay off financially falls between January 1 and July 16, when Jupiter transits Cancer, a water sign compatible with your earth-sign sun. This occurs in your solar third house of communication and travel. No telling what treasures you may discover during this transit. Perhaps your Web site wins an award. Or you sell your novel. Or you become a travel writer.

Good backup dates: October 26 to December 4, when Mars transits fellow earth sign Capricorn, your solar ninth house. Your ambitions lead you in new directions—perhaps overseas, into publishing, or higher education. Maybe law school is in your future!

Gemini

Left to your own devices, things like checkbooks and saving accounts and IRAs and investments are for other people to ponder, such as your accountant, partner, parents, or sibling. You would rather write and talk about *ideas*. So let's talk about the *idea* of money. What does it actually represent to you? Energy? Freedom? Albatross? During 2014 it's to your advantage to look at money as energy and freedom. The more you make, the greater your freedom to do what interests you. The more effort you expend, the greater the energy you're putting into what you do and the greater the return. At least that's how it's supposed to work in theory. But you have to remain focused and resolute.

Most Geminis are versatile and adaptable, and many are excellent communicators. How can you use those particular skills and talents to earn an income?

One of your best times this year for increasing your earnings falls between January 1 and July 16, when Jupiter transits Cancer, your solar second house of finances. This transit has been going on since 2013, so by now you should have a clear idea how it works and the kind of luck and expansion that accompanies it.

Another excellent period for increasing your earnings occurs between June 23 and July 18, when Venus transits your sign. Things may seem to be going so well that you could be tempted to kick back and chill. Resist that temptation! Use this time frame to move forward—ask for a raise, apply for a promotion, or look for a new job that pays more.

An excellent backup period is September 13 to October 26, when Mars transits fire sign Sagittarius, your solar seventh house. This transit could bring exactly the right business partner you need. Or you and your spouse or partner go into business together.

Cancer

Your imagination and intuition should serve you well this year, particularly if you use both to expand your income. You tend to be good at budgeting your money and usually know what you earn, spend, and on what. Even though you probably aren't obsessed about money, you find a sense of security in having money in savings that you can draw on when you need to.

This year there are several periods that favor your finances. The first occurs between July 18 and August

12, when Venus transits your sign. During this period ask for a raise or promotion, apply for new jobs, network with professional peers, or open an IRA. Lucky you, this transit occurs just after the Mercury retrograde in your sign ends. Those dates: June 7 to July 1. Reread the section on Mercury retrogrades in chapter 2.

The second period when your finances—and just about everything else in your life—may undergo radical expansion occurs between January 1 and July 16, while expansive Jupiter transits your sign. This transit has been going on since last June, so you undoubtedly have a good idea already about the kinds of events and opportunities that Jupiter often brings.

Excellent backup dates: August 12 to September 5, when Venus transits Leo and your financial area. This period could bring a new source of income.

Leo

In 2014 the secret to staying afloat financially is twofold. First, have the facts at your fingertips. Know how much you actually bring home after taxes and FICA and any other fees that are automatically deducted from your income. Can you live on your take-home pay? If not, where can you cut back in your budget? Do you and your partner eat out frequently? Is it necessary? Do you go on shopping sprees? Keep track of your expenses for a couple of weeks for a more accurate picture of what comes in—and goes out.

Second, as one of the most flamboyant and theatrical signs of the zodiac, you probably like to look your best when in public. Be sure to budget for that—

clothing, shoes, hairstylists, spas—whatever it takes to maintain your public persona. But instead of shopping at the upscale shops, perhaps you can do equally well in thrift stores.

There are some excellent periods in 2014 for increasing your earnings. The first period falls between August 12 and September 5, when Venus transits your sign. This one boosts self-confidence, other people find you infinitely appealing, and you can do no wrong, Leo. So ask for a raise or promotion or send out résumés. Unexpected bonuses or royalties could arrive during this time. If so, stash the money in an IRA.

The next period falls between July 16, 2014, and August 11, 2015, when Jupiter transits your sign. Expansive Jupiter seeks to improve your life in all areas during this transit.

Excellent backup dates: September 5 to 29, when Venus moves through Virgo, your financial area. This period favors details and enables you to connect all the dots.

Virgo

You're the most discriminating of signs—measured, diligent, with a penchant for details. You can be something of a perfectionist too, but rarely demand of others what you demand of yourself. Whatever you take on, you do so with complete dedication. So in 2014 perfect your finances, Virgo. Set your monetary goals and then figure out how best to achieve them.

One of the most favorable periods for earning more falls between September 5 and 29, when Venus transits your sign. This period is favorable for landing a raise or promotion, for receiving money from unexpected sources—an insurance payment, a royalty check—and for sending out résumés for a job that pays you more. It's also good for pitching manuscripts and screenplays.

Another potentially profitable period occurs between January 1 and July 16, when expansive Jupiter transits compatible water sign Cancer and forms a beneficial angle to your sun. Friends and any groups to which you belong prove helpful. This period is when you're in the right place at the right time to bolster your bank account, land a raise, or make money by expanding your services or products to overseas markets.

Excellent backup dates: September 29 to October 23, when Venus transits Libra, your financial area.

Libra

Your sign, like Taurus, is Venus ruled, so its transits are particularly important to you. You feel more comfortable and balanced when surrounded by beauty—fresh flowers, art, pleasing furniture, perhaps even some sort of unique collection that has good memories attached to it. Music and books may be important to you too, and perhaps some of your disposable income goes toward these things.

Between September 29 and October 23 Venus transits your sign. This period should be particularly good for you. Venus is happy in your sign and can help you to bring in additional income from a variety of different sources. If you're in sales, you can sell anything to anyone. You might sell a manuscript, piece of art, or some other product born of your creativity.

During Jupiter's transit of compatible fire sign Leo, between July 16, 2014, and August 11, 2015, you may experience an expansion in your income that seems to happen without any effort on your part. That's an illusion, of course. You have been seeding the possibilities for quite a while now. Jupiter means expansion, and its energy can be used wherever you apply your attention and energy.

Excellent backup dates: March 1 to May 19, when Mars is in direct motion in your sign. This one acts like a booster rocket!

Scorpio

As a fixed water sign and the most emotionally intense sign in the zodiac, you're no stranger to transformation. With Pluto as the ruler of your sign, your life is constantly undergoing transformation of some kind. But if you would like to bolster and transform your finances, 2014 is a great year to do it. Your considerable intuition and ability to get to the absolute bottom line of anything you research and investigate serve you well this year.

Between October 23 and November 16 Venus transits your sign. So during this period ask for a raise, apply for a promotion, or send out résumés for jobs that really interest you. Be proactive. You and your ideas appeal to others. Your charisma intrigues them, so use it to your advantage.

Another excellent period for expanding your income occurs between January 1 and July 16, 2014, when Jupiter transits fellow water sign Cancer and forms a beneficial angle to your sun. This period should be productive for you, with new creative opportunities that could bring in additional income.

Saturn begins the year in your sign, Scorpio, which should bring stability and structure to your finances and other areas of your life. It's retrograde between March 2 and July 20, so it essentially enters a dormant state during this period. But before the retrograde and afterward, until it enters Sagittarius on December 23, use its energy to build a more solid financial foundation for yourself.

Excellent backup dates: July 25 to September 13, when Mars, your coruler, transits your sign. This one is your booster rocket and confers enormous physical energy and resolve.

Sagittarius

Let the good times roll ... and roll! As a mutable fire sign, your life is about activity and forward motion. You don't have time for things like budgets, balancing a checkbook, and keeping track of what you earn and spend. Then when it's time to do your taxes, you freak out. You can't find receipts, your files are messed up ... you get the idea.

In 2013 we advised you to organize your finances. If you did that, in 2014 your finances should be much easier to navigate. You'll be alert for the periods when it will be easier to increase your income. More money means more travel, and any Sadge loves that idea!

Between November 16 and December 10 Venus transits your sign. Not only does your self-confidence soar, but others find you appealing and want you on their team. So ask for a raise or promotion, pitch your ideas, or submit your manuscript or screenplay or some other product you have created.

Between January 31 and March 5 and December 10, 2014, and January 4, 2015, Venus in direct motion transits Capricorn, your financial area. These two periods should prompt you to be careful with your money, particularly as your income increases. Just because you have more money in your pocket, Sadge, doesn't mean it should go out as quickly as it comes in. Capricorn is a grounded, focused sign, and as Venus moves through it you learn the wisdom of saving.

Another excellent period for you and your money should occur during Jupiter's thirteen-month transit through fellow fire sign Leo. This one should increase not only your finances but also opportunities in whatever area you place your attention.

Capricorn

As a cardinal earth sign, you build your financial world just as you do everything else, one brick at a time. You do it patiently, methodically, and usually have a goal in mind—double your earnings in six months, for instance. Or pay off your mortgage in the next two years.

In 2014 you have several windows of opportunity when it's easier to increase your earnings, launch a business, pitch an idea that someone will buy, or sell a book. Luck is on your side; you're in the right place at the right time; you meet exactly the right people who make things happen. The first period falls between January 31 and March 5; the second period is between December 10, 2014, and January 4, 2015, when Venus is moving direct through your sign. This transit is a confidence booster. When you feel good about yourself, others pick up on it, and suddenly everything flows your way. If you're looking for a better-paying job or a second job, then this period could bring news.

The second period occurs between January 1 and July 16 when Jupiter transits your opposite sign, Cancer. This transit should expand your professional partnerships, which in turn could be very positive for your finances.

You have an additional plus this year. Saturn is in Scorpio until December 23, forming a strong and beneficial angle to your sun. This transit helps you to build solid financial foundations.

Aquarius

You don't really fit into any financial category. Some Aquarians are great with money; others aren't. Some are savers; others are spenders. But one thing is for sure. When you make up your mind to do something, you do it. No one and nothing can sway you from a path you've chosen. So for 2014 let's look at times when your income can increase.

One of the most favorable periods falls between March 5 and April 5. Venus transits your sign, suggesting that your appeal is broad and others like you and your ideas, making this an ideal time to ask for a raise. Ask with the expectation that the raise will be given. Whether you're sending out résumés or interviewing for jobs, you're in your element and should reap the rewards you so justly deserve.

Another good period falls between April 5 and

May 2, when Venus moves through Pisces, your financial area. You may have a tough time making up your mind if you're given choices about your money. But once you do make up your mind, this transit could bring about a raise, result in the repayment of a loan, or perhaps bring in an insurance payment or tax break.

Excellent backup dates: December 4, 2014, to January 12, 2015. Mars is in your sign, and it's your booster rocket, Aquarius.

Pisces

Your considerable imagination and intuition will prove enormously valuable in this year of transformation. Whatever you can imagine, after all, can manifest itself. So if you're imagining a quantum leap in your income, Pisces, fix a figure firmly in mind, focus on it, release it—and let the universe figure out the connections that must be made for you to earn that amount of money.

In the interim, of course, it's smart not to just sit back but to become more proactive. If you dislike your job, figure out what you would like to be doing and start submitting applications and résumés. If you often find yourself short of money, set up a realistic budget and try to stick to it. You know, do the small stuff!

Timing is essential, so let's take a look at the windows of opportunity in 2014 when things really flow your way. These periods are when you should ask for a raise or promotion, submit résumés, schedule interviews, do whatever you can to earn more. The first period falls between April 5 and May 2, when Venus transits your sign. This is when you're more you than ever! Turn on the charm, let your muse in 24/7.

The second period falls between January 1 and July 16, when expansive Jupiter transits fellow water sign Cancer and forms a beneficial angle to your sun. Expansion, luck, you're in the right place at the right time!

CHAPTER 5

Lunar Madness in 2014

Collective Concepts of the Moon

There is something truly magical about the moon. As the closest celestial body to Earth, it has captured man's imagination for millennia. It has been the stuff of myths and fairy tales, poetry and legends. It has been worshipped and cursed and endowed with magical and curative powers. Religions have grown up around it. Sacrifices have been made to it.

In ancient cultures the passage of time was marked according to the lunation—or cycle—of the moon. A *month* was the time between one new moon and the next, and in a typical year there were thirteen lunar cycles. This way of marking time still exists among some pagan sects and may be closer to our natural rhythms than our present solar calendar.

Early shamans may have timed certain rituals according to the phases of the moon. Tribal people often planted crops during a new moon and harvested at a full moon. In the eighth century B.C. various civilizations discarded their 360-day calendar and based the calendar on observations of the sky. In ancient Rome priests observed the heavens and were supposed to announce to the emperor when a new month began. The month usually began with a new moon. This practice was also used by the Celts and Babylonians.

In the early fifties the moon was a favorite theme in science fiction books and movies, and the storylines rarely varied: the aliens came from the moon, we colonized the moon, or the moon fell out of orbit . . . you get the general picture. Even Disney issued movies in which the moon played a vital role. In one film, a Western, a woman who wore a hoop skirt typical of the American west started bouncing and kept bouncing higher and higher until she bounced right into the moon. The shadow you see in the moon is, according to Disney, that woman in the hoop skirt.

In 1969 Neil Armstrong took one giant leap for mankind, and our concept of the moon was forever changed. Even though its relative position in the sky hadn't changed, everything else about it had.

We now had some idea what it really looked like, and the news was far from good. Dust, dust, and more dust. A black vacuum. Unimaginable cold. Nothingness. What's most vivid in our minds, though, is how the Earth looked from the moon—a swirling turquoise gem 240,000 miles distant, a blue pearl turning in space. Our planet literally looked alive.

This was the year when Vietnam was in full swing. Americans arrived home in body bags, riots swept across college campuses, LSD was the drug of choice. People were tuning in and dropping out faster than the pictures of the moon were beamed back to earth.

This was the year that half a million people converged on the tiny town of Woodstock, New York, to hear Hendrix, Baez, Dylan, Joplin, and all the other musicians who had captured the emotional reality of war and chaos. Women threw off their shackles. Carlos Castaneda and Aldous Huxley hurled open the doors to other realities. Camelot was dead, Martin Luther King was dead, and we had walked on the moon.

In many ways those steps of Armstrong's signaled that we were ready to confront our unconscious selves, our feminine, intuitive selves.

Fast-forward to the summer of 1997, July 4 to be exact. In the opening scenes of the movie *Independence Day* a mammoth shadow falls across the surface of the moon. A moving shadow whose shape is unmistakable. The message comes through loud and clear: the shadow is that of a spaceship that uses the moon as a base, and now that ship is on the move toward Earth. What ensues is pure Hollywood, with Will Smith holding the record for aliens annihilated. But *Independence Day*, like Armstrong's one giant leap, is part of our contemporary, collective perceptions of the moon, its essential beauty and sublime mysteries.

Despite Hollywood and NASA, each of us has some personal concept about the moon. After all, we drop our heads back on any given night, and there it is, shaped like a ubiquitous eye or the grin of a Cheshire cat or like a piece of fruit with the top lopped off. It speaks to us. We speak to it. Romance, madness, werewolves, witches, pagans, Druids, ocean tides and blood tides, or a sharp rise in murder and mayhem: it's all fair game where the moon is concerned. Every notion that we hold about the moon is true *for us,* and that subjective texture is certainly in keeping with the nature of the moon in astrology.

If the sun is where you shine in your corner of the universe, the moon is your personal oracle. If the sun represents your life force, the moon represents the internal landscape that supports and maintains the life force. In astrology lunar energy is embodied in that mythological moment when Luke Skywalker recognizes that Darth Vader is his father or when, in *ET,* the alien is getting drunk and the boy is trying to dissect a frog at school and their psyches mesh. Lunar energy is operating when reality splits off for the character Gwyneth Paltrow plays in *Sliding Doors* or during the love scene in *Titanic.*

Lunar energy is the MO in *Thelma and Louise, Jacob's Ladder,* and *What Dreams May Come.* It's the psychic visions the young boy has in *The Shining* or the visions another young boy has in *The Sixth Sense.* It's the mother's anguish in *The Deep End of the Ocean.* Without lunar energy we would be empty shells, automatons, the burn-the-books society in *Fahrenheit 451.* We would be Keanu Reeves still stuck in the matrix, powerless puppets who accept everything at face value.

Lunar Facts and Oddities

Most of us learn facts about the moon in grade-school science class. Today's kids have a distinct advantage over their parents of course because we've already been to the moon, and information is so readily accessible through the Internet.

The moon is our only satellite, and its average distance from Earth is 238,857 miles. Its revolution around the Earth takes twenty-seven days, seven hours, and forty-three minutes. Even though it's only a quarter the size of Earth, its gravitational pull is the main cause of our ocean tides. In fact, the moon actually has more than twice the effect on tides than the sun.

Since our bodies are primarily water, the moon's gravitational pull on the tides also affects our bodily fluids, metabolic rates, and of course our emotions. The link, for instance, between the full moon and violent aggression has been noted for years by police officers, hospital workers, and employees at mental institutions.

In the 1970s a Miami psychiatrist, Arnold Lieber, decided to conduct a scientific study to find out if these observations were true. As a med student at Jackson Memorial Hospital in Miami he'd noticed recurring periods when patients on the psyche ward were more disturbed than usual. These periods would last for several days, then the patients would resume their normal behavior. He became curious about the phenomenon and finally conducted a scientific study. His findings, later backed by four other independent studies, confirmed that during the full moon and, to a lesser extent, the new moon, there are increases in all violent crimes—homicide, rape, assault. There's also an increase in lesser crimes—burglary, auto theft, larceny, and drunken and disorderly behavior.

Is it any coincidence, then, that the word *lunatic* is derived from the word *lunar*?

Hospital workers and maternity ward nurses have

long noticed that more babies are born at the full and new moons than at any other time of the month. These may be due to the fact that the gravitational pull is strongest when the moon, sun, and Earth are aligned, as they are during the new and full moons. These observations have been backed by scientific studies. Interestingly enough, the lunar calendar is still the basis for calculating a pregnancy. The nine months are synodic months (the length of time it takes the moon to orbit Earth).

Since the moon has no atmosphere, it has nothing to protect it from meteor strikes, which is why its surface is pocked with impact craters. Since it has no tectonic or volcanic activity, its surface is immune to the erosive effects of atmospheric weathering, tectonic shifts, and volcanic upheavals that reshape the surface of our planet. In comparison, Earth is a work in progress. On the moon, even the footprints left by the Apollo astronauts will remain intact for millions of years unless a meteor strike obliterates them.

The moon's gravity is about a sixth of ours; that's why the Apollo astronauts looked like they were jumping rope up there. Despite appearances to the contrary, the moon has no light of its own. That gorgeous full moon you see each month is the reflected light of our sun.

Astrological Lunar Facts

The moon in your horoscope is every bit as important as your sun sign. In fact, Eastern astrologers give the moon greater emphasis than the sun sign. The moon rules the sign of Cancer and the fourth house in the horoscope. It represents mom or whoever plays that role for you and also symbolizes other women in your life. The moon is feminine, yin, our intuitive selves.

In the physical body her territory pertains primarily to women—breasts, ovaries, womb. In both genders she rules internal fluids and the stomach, and of course she's our emotional barometer, the gauge of our inner health. Not surprisingly, the moon rules conception.

A Czech physician, in fact, theorized that every woman had a fertility cycle that depended on the phase of the moon when she was born. Eugene Jones developed a fertilization calendar based on his theory, which allegedly showed a 98 percent success rate. He charged an astronomical fee for his calendar, but people who were desperate for children paid it.

Jones claimed that if a woman used his methods, she could choose the gender of her child. His technique was based on the rules of classical astrology, which he'd studied, and boils down to using the gender of moon signs. If conception took place on a Leo day, the child would be male. On a Taurus day, the child would be a girl.

The medical establishment went berserk over his claims. But when a panel of gynecologists challenged him to predict the genders of babies based only on their conception dates, Jones' accuracy was 87 percent.

If you don't know the sign of your natal moon, check on any of the astrology sites listed in this book and get a free birth chart. You'll need your exact time of birth, place, and of course the date!

The Transiting Moon

The moon changes signs every two and a half days. As you follow along in the daily prediction section for your sign, you'll be able to keep tabs on where the moon is on any given day. In the daily predictions we note when the moon is new or full. New moons favor new beginnings. Quite often around the time of the new moon you may receive good news about a project, relationship, or a financial or family matter. Full moons often coincide with completions, culminations, and news that ties up loose ends.

Certain activities are favored on certain lunar days, so let's take a look at how you can maximize the transiting moon's energy in your life.

Aries Moon

Cardinal Fire Sign

This is the day to be a fearless entrepreneur, to move forward on projects that have been sitting on the back burner for weeks or months. It's a great time to initiate new projects too, especially those that have been rattling around in the back of your head for some time.

You may feel restless and impatient with others, so the best way to deal with it is to pour that energy into something about which you feel passionate. Others see you as a leader, as the person with answers. You attract individuals who are eager to be on your team. You feel more self-sufficient, capable of doing whatever needs to be done.

Follow your impulses regardless of how odd they may seem. Sometimes our impulses are the universe's way of leading us toward a new opportunity, relationship, or creative project. Since Mars rules Aries, physical activity is heightened. Take a yoga class. Join the gym. Go walking. Weather permitting, it's a great day for a hike, bike ride, or long swim.

It's a good day to *believe* that whatever you desire can manifest itself. Your intentions and focus are key.

Taurus Moon

Fixed Earth Sign

The moon loves Taurus as much as it loves Cancer, the sign that it rules. In Taurus lunar energies work effortlessly and smoothly, and that makes your intuition easier to develop and use.

On a Taurus moon day think about that children's story *Ferdinand the Bull.* The author probably wasn't thinking about Taurus when he created the character, but Ferdinand is the perfect archetype for Taurus. Ferdinand enjoyed peaceful surroundings, and today so do you. In fact, peacefulness and harmony are vital to your emotional well-being. You need these qualities the way a Gemini moon needs books or education or communication with other people.

It will take a lot to anger you today, but repeated provocation can trigger your "bull's rush" fury, the human equivalent of Ferdinand's reaction to the bee sting. Some of the things that can set you off are incessant nagging by someone who wants you to do something you don't want to do, insistence that you act in a particular way, unreasonable demands or actions by anyone.

A Taurus moon day enables you to stick with something right to the end. You won't be a quitter. You will also be slow to change your mind and opinion and won't be rushed or cajoled into doing something that doesn't interest you.

If you enjoy gardening or have a particular artistic passion, then today is the day to indulge!

Gemini Moon

Mutable Air Sign

Today your nemesis is boredom. Its possibility unnerves you. If you were put in a bare room without windows, books, TV, radio, computer, paper or pen, phone, fax, or anything else, you would freak within the hour. This may be true of the other air-sign moons as well, but for the Gemini moon it's a sure thing. Your emotional well-being needs mental stimulation and the means to communicate with others.

It's a good day to start blogging, if you haven't already, to dust off that old manuscript you were working on way back when, or to get together with friends and shoot the breeze. You may feel compelled to sign up for a workshop or even an online course in something that interests you. Or you may decide to go to college or graduate school. It's a great day for research, for delving into a topic or concern and finding out everything you can about it.

Communication, whatever form is takes, is paramount.

Cancer Moon

Cardinal Water Sign

Today your memories work overtime. You're able to conjure sights, smells, tastes, sounds, and textures from your past in vivid detail. The event you're recalling may have happened thirty years ago, but in your memory it's just as fresh and detailed as the day it happened.

The moon rules Cancer, so it's at home in this sign. This is where its energies express themselves most smoothly. Today your emotions are racing through you, and it may be easy to have your feelings hurt. Your acute sensitivity makes you feel vulnerable, and it isn't easy for you to step back and view a situation or relationship dispassionately.

Family, home, and roots are especially important to you today. Schedule time to be with the people you love. Whether it's a traditional family or friends whom you love like family, you draw comfort and sustenance from these individuals. It's a good time to work on creative projects; your inspiration comes from deep places within you. During the Cancer moon you may have a real soft spot for animals—strays that drop by your place for a bowl of food, the neighbor's cat that sneaks into your house. A visit to your local pound may be in order!

Leo Moon

Fixed Fire Sign

It's a perfect day to showcase your talents. In fact when you enter a room, people notice you. If for some reason they don't, you make sure that they do. This isn't just an ego thing, either. Applause and being noticed are vital to your well-being today even if your only audience is your family. *You need to be recognized as someone special.*

Your flair for drama today is remarkable. It runs throughout everything you do—from the way you dress, speak, and act to the activities in which you engage. You may decide to take in a play or try out for a part. Creatively you're at the top of your game, and anything you undertake will bear this dramatic stamp.

It's a good time to spend time with your kids doing something everyone enjoys, volunteer at an animal shelter, get out and be seen, socialize, make new contacts. Network. Be as flamboyant as you can imagine.

Virgo Moon

Mutable Earth Sign

Today you're in a quest for perfection, and the words *Be the best that you can* take on a whole new dimension of meaning. You thrive on order and manage to use today's lunar energy to tackle emotional chaos in your life and impose order on it.

Virgo tends to be a health-oriented sign, so today favors starting a new diet, nutritional program, or exercise regimen. Even if you're already involved in these areas, consider fine-tuning the details. You also may want to consider blogging or writing about what you're learning about health, nutrition, and exercise.

Today also favors performing a service for someone else—not for pay, not with any thought of compensation, but as a good deed. This could mean anything from volunteering at your favorite charity to putting in some time at an animal rescue sanctuary. Pay attention to your spiritual beliefs today. Are you in tune with a greater good? Are your thoughts the most positive they can be?

Libra Moon

Cardinal Air Sign

Among astrologers certain moon signs stir the soul for the sheer beauty of what they represent. The Taurus moon is one of these. The Libra moon is another.

Today at the heart of it you're a lover, a true romantic. Moonlit beaches, bouquets of roses, books of poetry, going to the opera, a summer rain: this is the language your soul speaks during the Libra moon. So first of all surround yourself with beauty today— music, scenery, people. Just the sight of all this beauty will deepen your appreciation for life.

It's a good day for group work—in your community or with your students, peers, or fellow workers. Or it's a great time to socialize and network. Today your interests tend toward people and relationships, your artistic interests, and attaining peace and harmony. You can see both sides of an issue with greater clarity, and try to avoid conflict.

The Libra moon can enhance your intuition, so try to follow your hunches today and see where they lead you. If you don't meditate yet, today is a terrific time to start. It doesn't have to be lengthy. In fact, five minutes in a quiet place, with your mind still, is all you need. You'll come out of it refreshed. Keep track of any impressions that come your way during those five minutes.

If you're in a committed relationship, be sure to take time today to spend time with your partner. Have a romantic dinner at home or at your favorite restaurant. Talk, converse, get in touch with each other.

Scorpio Moon

Fixed Water Sign

Emotionally it's a powerful day. You feel everything so intensely that it's as if some new, inner part of you has awakened from a deep sleep. You may feel as if you've been seized by a force beyond your control. Despite how it feels, this sense of outside forces is just an illusion. Your emotions are your most powerful allies today. They provide you with a direct, immediate connection to the deepest parts of your intuitive self and are capable of instantly transforming your reality.

This transformation happens when you bring your considerable will, intent, and desire to bear against whatever it is that you want to change. When the energy of this moon is focused and backed with passion, this change occurs at the quantum level and can result in the remission of illness or disease, sudden rise in wealth and fame, an explosion of psychic ability . . . well, you get the general idea.

Scorpio is also about power—the power we wield over others and the power others wield over us. All too often this lunar energy is misused or abused when it concerns power issues; then its tremendous capacity for positive transformation becomes negative. The difference seems to be self-awareness.

It's a great day to work with healing energies, intuitive and psychic development, and research and investigation.

Sagittarius Moon

Mutable Fire Sign

Oh, baby, let the good times roll! And for the Sagittarian moon, those good times mean music, deep talk, exotic travel, esoteric ideas. Today you're an explorer. Those explorations may take you to the farther ends of the Earth or deep within the mysteries of the universe. In one way or another this moon enables you to search for the higher truth, the larger picture, a more expansive perspective.

You may be more blunt than usual when dealing with people today, particularly when the other guy just doesn't get what seems so obvious to you. Patience and nuance aren't your strong points during this period. The exception to this occurs when you're pursuing something about which you feel passionate, then you have the patience of Mother Teresa and are as detail oriented as a Virgo.

You're called to action today. You would rather do than think about doing. As a mutable sign, you're emotionally adaptable. You have opinions about virtually everything and aren't the least bit hesitant in expressing these opinions. This becomes a problem if you're dogmatic or bombastic about what you believe and try to convert others to your way of thinking. So today strive to nurture patience and optimism.

Capricorn Moon

Cardinal Earth Sign

The moon isn't particularly comfortable in this sign. It chafes at all the rules and restrictions that Capricorn seeks to impose and dislikes all that earthy grounding. However, this moon certainly favors strategy—laying out goals and figuring ways to achieve them. Your physical energy is excellent today and enables you to work long hours to meet a deadline, regardless of whether that deadline is self-imposed (which it often is) or imposed by a boss.

You feel quite independent today and may find yourself outdoors, hiking alone through the wilderness, or at the gym, putting in extra time on the treadmill. Under this lunar influence you push yourself, move the bar higher, and feel a certain determination to carve your niche in the larger world.

Today it's easier to categorize your emotions, to look at things dispassionately. So tackle stuff that pushes your buttons, issues that you've pushed aside but which beg for a resolution.

Aquarius Moon

Fixed Air Sign

Today you march to a different drummer. You may hear a different kind of music in your very cells and feel compelled to decipher the message and act on it.

This is the sign, after all, that ushers in new paradigms by refusing to go along with the status quo.

The visionary component to this moon sign gives you an edge today on new trends. You can spot the next wave long before anyone else does. The trick is acting on it and putting it to work for you in your personal and professional life. Your rational mind may try to intervene, to argue and put up blocks, to keep you within the confining box of consensus reality. Or someone close to you—a parent, close friend, significant other—inadvertently plays that role, and you suddenly find yourself on the defensive.

So today be fearless; go forward secure in the knowledge that your vision is correct!

Pisces Moon

Mutable Water Sign

Today you're the archetypal dreamer, your feet never really firmly rooted on the earth. You're deeply compassionate today too, a true bleeding heart. You probably won't be able to pass a homeless person on the street without giving him money, and you definitely won't resist the soulful gaze of a stray pup or kitten. Injustices of any sort may fill you with a deep sadness. Your challenge during this moon is to detach emotionally from situations and people who cause you this kind of anguish.

Part of the problem is that today you're a psychic sponge who soaks up the emotions and moods of the people around you. This alone makes it vital that you associate with upbeat, positive people and situations that boost your energy rather than sap it.

The Pisces moon favors imagination, intuition, and any artistic endeavor. On a strictly mundane level it's a fine day to shop for new clothes, get a new hairdo, or redesign yourself in some way. Also, your dreams should be especially vivid and could contain important insights and information.

Eclipses

Every year there are at least four eclipses—two solar, two lunar. Solar eclipses are like double new moons; the opportunities are twice as powerful and delicious. They usually involve external events. Lunar eclipses are about internal events and emotions. Eclipses always come in pairs and form an axis of energy. If there's a solar eclipse in Aries, for example, about two weeks later there will be a lunar eclipse in Libra, the opposite sign of Aries.

When an eclipse falls in your sun, moon, or rising sign, you will feel the effects quite powerfully. Be sure to check out the Big Picture chapter for your sign, where we talk about the year's eclipses.

CHAPTER 6

Mars in 2014

Mars rules fire sign Aries and corules Scorpio. It takes two years to circle the zodiac and spends about two months in a sign. Think of this planet as the action hero of the zodiac, the one who is always on the move, doing, acting, getting things done, your personal warrior.

The sign and house placement for your natal Mars describes how you use your physical energy, your desire for personal achievement, and the nature of your sexuality. First check out one of the astrology sites listed in the book and find out the sign and house placement for your natal Mars. Then find your natal Mars in the descriptions below.

Mars in Aries or in the First House

Since Mars rules this sign, the planet is happy here and functions at optimum levels. If your natal Mars is in Aries, you go after what you want; you are impulsive, sometimes reckless, and basically fearless. You're the one who loves the roller coasters at theme parks and hikes to the summit of Mount Everest and heads out for parts unknown with just a backpack and an ATM card.

You have a need to dominate your immediate environment, and your leadership ability is strong. But sometimes you may lack direction. You're terrific at initiating projects, but if you lose interest, you walk away without regret and leave what you started for someone else to complete.

Your sex drive is particularly strong and can sometimes manifest selfishly, with little regard for your partner. You could be somewhat accident prone.

Mars in Taurus or in the Second House

You aren't easily discouraged by obstacles of any kind. Your sheer determination and strength of will are well developed, but you may not use these attributes to their fullest. You take practical, purposeful action in everything you begin.

You pursue your financial goals with relentless energy and drive, but you may have trouble holding on to what you earn because you enjoy spending. Try to pay cash for your purchases so that you have a clearer grasp of how much money goes out.

Your sexual nature is sensuous, often passionate. You find pleasure through your profession.

Mars in Gemini or in the Third House

Your energy is expressed mentally and intellectually. You're an avid student—even once you're out of school. You tend to take on multiple projects simultaneously, which scatters your energy. Your mental restlessness needs a creative outlet, otherwise you can become argumentative.

You think well on your feet and make decisions quickly. Sometimes you can be so aggressive about communicating your ideas that you create unnecessary tension. With this placement there can be a lot of competition with siblings. Your challenge is to think before you speak. You pursue your goals well, but sometimes have so many goals that your energy is all over the place.

In terms of sexuality your mind has to be courted and seduced first!

Mars in Cancer or in the Fourth House

Your family life is active and emphasizes the development of individuality, competition, and independence. If you feel you have to dominate the domestic scene, that can sometimes be a source of tension.

Your experiences are filtered through a subjective lens. You may be the kind of person who takes everything personally, so it's difficult at times to be objective about issues that are important to you.

The intuitive component with this placement may give you an advantage in terms of your family. You simply have to tune in to find out what your kids are really doing! This intuitive connection also operates with your partner, parents, and anyone else who shares your domestic life.

Your sexuality is particularly heightened when you're emotionally in synch with your partner.

Mars in Leo or in the Fifth House

You're all about passion. It rushes through everything you do and say, even in the way you move. You have strong leadership abilities, are as fearless as Mars in Aries, and your will is powerful and determined. Artistic or musical skills are sometimes indicated with this placement.

You may be into competitive sports, enjoy strenuous physical activity, and are an ardent and considerate lover. You pursue romance and creative endeavors with equal passion, and with both the one thing you should be careful about is acting impulsively.

Your sexuality is powerful, and others pick up on that, so you have no shortage of people clamoring for your attention.

Mars in Virgo or in the Sixth House

Your energy finds expression through efficient, practical pursuits. You're one of the hardest workers around, especially when the work involves attention to details. You dislike laziness in others and may criticize them for it, but that usually gets you nowhere and doesn't change anything.

You pursue your goals with a quiet diligence, rarely giving up or surrendering to despair when something doesn't work out. Sooner or later you attain what you want.

In terms of sexuality you're quite discriminating and picky about what you want in a partner. But once you're smitten, you tend to be loyal.

Mars in Libra or in the Seventh House

Your energy finds its best expression in partnerships and through and with other people. Your marriage and partnerships are infused with energy and are a source of inspiration to you.

You can charm your way into any situation or relationship. You usually understand another person's point of view because you can put yourself in his or her shoes. You excel at diplomacy and seek harmony and peace in whatever you do.

Your sexuality is determined to a large extent on how romantic you feel. It's about *mood*—how your partner approaches you, talks to you, courts you.

Mars in Scorpio or in the Eighth House

Mars corules Scorpio, so the planet is happy here and functions well. Your drive and ambition are legendary among the people who know you. Even strangers notice something about you that's different, out of the ordinary. Your sexuality is important to you, and the intensity with which it's expressed can be intimidating to others.

This same intensity, however, makes you an excellent investigator and researcher. You're never satisfied with easy answers. You dig and dig, always looking for the absolute bottom line in everything you do.

In a marriage or partnership you're actively involved in joint finances. This could cause friction between you and your partner, but it's something you insist on.

This placement for Mars can be quite psychic. At the very least you may delve into metaphysics, experience past-life recall, or see things that others don't.

Mars in Sagittarius or in the Ninth House

Your energy is best expressed in competitive sports, travel, and adventure, and the study of different cultures, philosophies, and spiritual traditions. Mars in Sagittarius can denote a career in publishing or higher education or as a crusader, a New Age leader, or even as an evangelist. You have the courage to act on your convictions.

Your sexuality is passionate but impulsive. You can commit to a relationship, but only when your heart is truly captured. Otherwise you prefer to remain free and unfettered.

Mars in the ninth house often takes wanderlust to new levels. It isn't enough for you to take an annual vacation. You live to travel, explore, and delve into various philosophies and spiritual traditions first hand.

Mars in Capricorn or in the Tenth House

Your energy finds its best expression in your career and profession. You're a worker who sets goals and moves toward them with a strategy, a plan. You're organized and use your time efficiently. When you want something, nothing holds you back. You pursue it with a self-motivation that others find intimidating and remarkable.

You may keep a tight hold on your sexuality. You're guarded and cautious and may get involved with people who are older than you. You have to be deeply certain about a relationship before you commit fully to it.

As a workaholic, it's smart to kick back sometimes

and evaluate where you are and where you're going. You need down times, periods when you relax and recharge.

Mars in Aquarius or in the Eleventh House

Your energy is best expressed through honing your individuality. You participate in groups when those groups support your interests and passions, but otherwise you're a paragon of individuality. Sometimes your approach is so different from the mainstream that others think you're eccentric.

Mars in the eleventh house explores group participation in a deeper way than Mars in other houses. You take the initiative in forming friendships and joining groups, but always there's a purpose behind it. You excel at initiating projects and launching them.

Your sexuality is apt to be unemotional unless you're madly in love with your partner. That said, love and sex begin in the mind for you.

Mars in Pisces or in the Twelfth House

Your energy is primarily intuitive and emotional. You can be inconsistent in the way you try to achieve your goals, or you're able to intuitively pull together facets of a project and make them work.

Your sexuality is intimately tied to your emotions and intuition. The other person has to "feel" right to you; there has to be some sort of heart-centered connection. With Mars in the twelfth house there can be secrecy surrounding your sexuality and relationships.

Sometimes with this placement there's a need to

recognize the ways in which you are aggressive so that the aggression doesn't turn against you and create health problems.

Important Mars and Venus Combinations

If you have a copy of your birth chart, take a look at where both Mars and Venus are located. If they are in the same sign and house, it suggests your sexuality is central to your life. Your passionate nature propels you into many different types of relationships, and not all of them are positive.

Generally this combination indicates that you're extremely attractive to the opposite sex, are fortunate in financial matters, and have artistic ability. It means your passion can be poured into artistic endeavors.

If your natal Mars is three signs away from your natal Venus (Mars in Aries, Venus in Capricorn, for instance), you may find yourself in stormy romances, where you and your partner are rarely on the same page. You may use other people for sexual gratification—or you're used in this way. That's the worst case scenario. However, with a bit of temperance and balance added to the mix, this combination can lead to a relationship in which you maintain your independence, and you and your partner appreciate each other's differences.

When your natal Mars is two signs away from Venus (Mars in Taurus, Venus in Cancer) or four signs away (Mars in Taurus, Venus in Virgo), you get along very well with the opposite sex. Your romantic relationships, partnerships, and marriage are harmonious and satisfying. A lot of your energy goes into creative pursuits.

If your natal Mars is opposite Venus, romantic and sexual relationships can be difficult. You may have to deal with jealousy and other such dark feelings. Your aggression can be intimidating. In extreme cases there can be abuse in relationships.

Everything in your natal chart, however, is indicative only of potential. What you do with that potential is entirely up to you — and your free will.

CHAPTER 7

The Luck Factor in 2014—
Synchronicity

The word *synchronicity* was coined by Swiss psychiatrist Carl Jung, when he wrote the introduction to the Richard Wilhelm translation of the *I Ching*. In a nutshell synchronicity is a meaningful coincidence. It happens when inner and outer events come together in a way that is meaningful to the observer and can't be explained by cause and effect.

We've all experienced these events. You're thinking of a friend you haven't seen for years, and suddenly you get an invite from that person on Facebook. Or you're delayed on your way to work one morning, and when you finally arrive at your turnoff discover there was an accident at just about the time you would have driven through if you'd been on time.

Once you're aware that these incidents hold a deeper meaning, they tend to happen more frequently. As you begin to work with these synchronicities, deciphering their messages, you suddenly realize you're in the flow, in the right place at the right time.

The planet that can help us get into the flow—Jupiter—is also the planet that represents luck and

expansion, success, prosperity, growth, creativity, spiritual interests, higher education, and the law. It governs publishing, overseas travel, and foreign countries
and any of our dealings with them. This year it will be
moving through two signs. Between January 1 and
July 16 it will be transiting water sign Cancer. Between July 16 and August 11, 2015, it will be moving
through fire sign Leo.

Check out www.synchrosecrets.com for a description of the most common types of synchronicities and
how to decipher the messages. Sometimes the messages are obvious. But some synchronicities require
interpretation. You have to think symbolically.

Now let's take a look at how these transits might
attract more synchronicity and luck into your life.

Aries

If you aren't aware of synchronicity, your best time
this year for delving into this fascinating phenomenon
is between July 16 and August 11, 2015, when Jupiter
transits fellow fire sign Leo, your solar fifth house of
love, romance, and creativity.

Consider keeping a journal about your experiences
as the synchronicities occur. Or create a file on your
computer or iPad. Note what types of synchronicity
they are. Do they occur in clusters, with the same
name, word, or phrase happening repeatedly during a
relatively short period of time? Do your experiences
act as guidance, confirmation, warning?

It's easy for you to get into the flow, Aries. Just follow your impulses. They often lead you to exactly
where you need to be. Or if you have a hunch that you

should follow a particular course, by all means follow the hunch. If a dream provides what seems to be information about an issue that concerns you, be sure to consider this information before making a decision.

Jupiter's transit through Leo indicates that you're going to enjoy delving into the topic of synchronicity and that you and a romantic partner may undertake the exploration together. You should experience luck with your creative endeavors, with projects and opportunities coming to you seemingly out of the blue.

Between January 1 and July 16, when Jupiter is transiting Cancer, your luck is heightened when you use your intuition and may involve your home and domestic environment. You might be able to move into a larger home in a neighborhood that suits your family better. Your family might expand—a birth, a parent or relative moves in, a child moves back home. At each step of the way synchronicities may be happening, particularly if major life transitions are occurring.

Taurus

Your luck factor and your synchronicities should be strongest during Jupiter's transit through compatible water sign Cancer: January 1 to July 16. This transit occurs in your solar third house—your neighborhood/community, siblings and other relatives, education and short-distance travel. These areas of your life may seem particularly lucky, and synchronicities may revolve around these areas.

Since the third house also governs your conscious mind and communication abilities, you may be writing or blogging about your experiences. You might start a Web site or write a book about these experiences.

Consider keeping a journal about your experiences as the synchronicities occur. Or create a file on your computer or iPad. Note what types of synchronicity they are. Do they occur in clusters, with the same name, word, or phrase happening repeatedly during a relatively short period of time? Do your experiences act as guidance, confirmation, warning?

During Jupiter's transit through Leo between July 16, 2014, and August 11, 2015, your luck factor revolves around your home and domestic situation. If you're going through a major transition of some kind—a move, the birth of a child, a change in income—the synchronicities may come fast and furiously.

Gemini

Jupiter's transit through Leo will be the one that is most beneficial for you, your luck factor, and your experience of synchronicity. The dates again: July 16, 2014, to August 11, 2015. It occurs in your solar third house—your neighborhood/community, siblings and other relatives, education and short-distance travel. These areas of your life may seem particularly lucky, and synchronicities may revolve around these areas.

Since the third house also governs your conscious mind and communication abilities, you may be writing or blogging about your experiences. You might start a Web site or write a book about these experiences.

Consider keeping a journal about your experiences as the synchronicities occur. Or create a file on your computer or iPad. Note what types of synchronicity they are. Do they occur in clusters, with the same name, word, or phrase happening repeatedly during a relatively short period of time? Do your experiences act as guidance, confirmation, warning?

Jupiter's transit through Cancer between January 1 to July 16 occurs in your financial area. Expect your financial opportunities to expand tremendously. Your luck factor will revolve around money. Synchronicities will occur in areas where you need guidance, confirmation, or warning.

Cancer

Oh, lucky you! The Jupiter transit to anticipate occurs between January 1 and July 16, when the planet of expansion and luck transits your sign! Everything in your life should expand during this period. Opportunities drop in your lap, your finances probably improve, or you get married or start a new career or family. Your intuition is greatly enhanced during this transit, and you're able to create a rich psychic environment for synchronicity. Be sure to decipher the messages of these synchronicities; they hold valuable information for you.

Consider keeping a journal about your experiences as the synchros occur. Or create a file on your computer or iPad. Note what types of synchronicity they are. Do they occur in clusters, with the same name, word, or phrase happening repeatedly during a relatively short period of time? Do your experiences act as guidance, confirmation, warning?

The second Jupiter transit, through Leo, occurs in

your financial area. This is when your finances really benefit. You land a fat raise, find a new, better-paying job, get a hefty bonus, or pick the right stocks. Synchronicities during this period may revolve around money.

Leo

The first Jupiter transit this year, in Cancer, occurs in your solar twelfth house. The dates: January 1 to July 16.

This period brings heightened insights concerning your own psyche and unconscious. You may try therapy or take up meditation. Jupiter's transit through Cancer makes your unconscious more accessible to you in some way, and you discuss the process with others through a blog or Web site, by writing a book, or keeping a journal. You may even work this process into your professional life in some way. One purpose for this transit is to clear out the old to make way for the new when Jupiter enters your sign on July 16. You may be discarding beliefs that no longer serve your best interests or breaking longstanding habits. Relationships may end but new ones begin.

If you feel this is a period of major transitions for you, the synchronicities are likely to come fast and furiously, offering confirmation, warning, peeks at the future. You might, for instance, dream of someone you know you've never met—only to meet that same person the next day or a week later. Any seeds you sow during this transit will be beneficial down the line, Leo.

During the second transit, when Jupiter is in your

sign, everything in your life opens up. Your luck factor is at its highest, and synchronicities swirl so quickly through your life that you better have a way to record them!

Consider keeping a journal about your experiences as the synchronicities occur. Or create a file on your computer or iPad. Note what types of synchronicity they are. Do they occur in clusters, with the same name, word, or phrase happening repeatedly during a relatively short period of time? Do your experiences act as guidance, confirmation, warning?

Virgo

Between January 1 and July 16 your luck factor and synchronicity experiences revolve around friends, groups to which you belong, your network of friends and acquaintances, and how you can achieve your wishes and dreams. Heady stuff, right?

The contacts you make during this period will be valuable and will expand your dreams in some way. The types of synchronicities you experience could involve virtually anything. The universe has a way of knowing what you need—even if you don't! Be sure to decode the messages that come with these synchronicities; they could prove helpful as guidance and confirmation. Your precision and attention to detail during this time should aid you. Your particular mindset lends itself to solving puzzles and mysteries.

During the second Jupiter transit, which lasts about thirteen months, your personal unconscious expands. This period brings heightened insights concerning your own psyche and unconscious. You may try therapy or take up meditation. Jupiter's transit through Leo and your solar twelfth house makes your unconscious more accessible to you in some way. You may discuss the process with others through a blog or Web site, by writing a book, or keeping a journal. You may even work this process into your professional life in some way.

Libra

During the first six months of the year, while Jupiter transits water sign Cancer and the career area of your chart, your professional life expands tremendously. This period should be exciting, with your professional opportunities multiplying almost more quickly than you can keep up with. You'll be lucky professionally— you're the right person at the right time and place, that sort of lucky. You may change jobs or careers, and if you do, it's for a better position and more pay. You could also be promoted or may decide to launch your own business.

Synchronicity will act as your guide, confirm your hunches, provide warnings or caution, or urge you to move full steam ahead. This period will enable you to make significant professional strides.

The second Jupiter transit, through Leo, occurs between July 16, 2014, and August 11, 2015. It happens in the area of your chart that governs friendships, groups, and your wishes and dreams. The contacts you make during this period will be valuable and expand your dreams in some way. The types of synchronicities you experience could involve virtually anything. The universe has a way of knowing what you need—even if you don't! Be sure to decode the messages that come with these synchronicities; they could prove helpful as guidance and confirmation.

Scorpio

During Jupiter's transit through Cancer, your solar ninth house, between January 1 and July 16 your opportunities and luck factor expand considerably.

The ninth house governs your worldview, higher education, publishing, and foreign travel, so expansions are likely to take place in those areas. Your communication opportunities should expand as well. You might sell a book or novel you've written, go to college or graduate school, or sign up for a seminar or workshop on a topic about which you're passionate. If you travel a great deal during this period, don't be surprised if you begin to experience a flurry of synchronicities.

Your spiritual beliefs will expand too. You may sample different religions or spiritual beliefs, launch a spiritual quest, or even travel to far-flung locales in search of spiritual truths. It all depends, Scorpio, on what you're seeking and how sincere you are in your desires.

Between July 16, 2014, and August 11, 2015, Jupiter transits Leo, your career area, and your professional life expands tremendously. This period should be exciting, with your professional opportunities multiplying almost more quickly than you can keep up with. You'll be lucky professionally—you're the right person at the right time and place, that sort of lucky. You may change jobs or careers, and if you do, it's for a better position and more pay. You could also be promoted or may decide to launch your own business. During this year you have many opportunities to show off your talents and skills.

Consider keeping a journal about your experiences as the synchros occur. Or create a file on your computer or iPad. Note what types of synchronicity they are. Do they occur in clusters, with the same name, word, or phrase happening repeatedly during a relatively short period of time? Do your experiences act as guidance, confirmation, warning?

Sagittarius

Since Jupiter rules your sign, its movements impact you quite personally and powerfully. Between January 1 and July 16 it transits Cancer, your solar eighth house. Your partner's income will expand, and you may be delving more deeply into metaphysics. Your intuitive abilities should deepen considerably under this transit. You may be researching and investigating life after death, communication with spirits, haunted houses, or things that go bump in the night. You'll be fortunate with mundane things as well—mortgages, loans, taxes, insurance, all of which falls under the eighth house. Synchronicities swirl in these areas. You're being guided.

The second transit, between July 16, 2014, and August 11, 2015, occurs in Leo, your solar ninth house. The ninth house governs your worldview, higher education, publishing, and foreign travel, so expansions are likely to take place in those areas. Your communication opportunities should expand as well. You might sell a book or novel you've written, go to college or graduate school, or sign up for a seminar or workshop on a topic about which you're passionate. You'll travel a lot during this period and should experience a flurry of synchronicities.

Your spiritual beliefs will expand too. You may sample different religions or spiritual beliefs, launch a spiritual quest, or even travel to far-flung locales on a spiritual quest of some kind.

Capricorn

During the first six months of the year, while Jupiter transits your opposite sign, Cancer, your partnership opportunities expand tremendously, and there's a strong element of luck to both professional and personal partnerships. You could find exactly the right person for a particular job or as a business partner. You and your partner may decide to move in together or get engaged or married. Be alert for synchronicities in every area of your life, and try to interpret the message and follow the guidance these meaningful coincidences provide.

The second Jupiter transit, between July 16, 2014, and August 11, 2015, occurs in Leo, your solar eighth house. The eighth house dynamics are always intriguing. On one side you have mundane issues—taxes, insurance, bank loans and mortgages—and on the other side you have esoteric stuff—hauntings, life after death, communication with the dead. These issues will be focal points for expansion. Synchronicities are likely to abound in these areas.

It should be easier for you to obtain a mortgage

and bank loan, and you will find yourself drawn to explore things that go bump in the night. You may even travel abroad to investigate crop circles or UFO reports. It all depends on how far outside the box your interests extend.

Aquarius

Between January 1 and July 16 Jupiter transits Cancer, your solar sixth house. The strong intuitive component to this transit helps you make better decisions in your daily work life and in regard to the maintenance of your health. You could land a promotion with more responsibility—and a raise that matches that responsibility—or hire more employees for your company. Regardless, a Jupiter transit usually brings expansion of some kind.

Synchronicities are likely to occur if major life transitions are going on—a move, job or career change, a birth or death in the family, a change in income.

Between July 16, 2014, and August 11, 2015, Jupiter transits Leo, your opposite sign. Your partnership opportunities expand tremendously, and there's a strong element of luck to both professional and personal partnerships. You could find exactly the right person for a particular job or as a business partner. You and your partner may decide to move in together or get engaged or married. Be alert for synchronicities in every area of your life, and try to interpret the message and follow the guidance these meaningful coincidences provide.

Pisces

Jupiter's transit through fellow water sign Cancer between January 1 and July 16 occurs in your solar fifth house—romance, love, creativity! You've got the Midas touch now and synchronicity is your middle name. You may feel you're being led into certain creative endeavors. Luck is on your side. Sounds like a recipe for paradise, doesn't it?

Between July 16, 2014, and August 11, 2015, Jupiter transits Leo, your solar sixth house. This thirteen-month transit should expand your daily work routine and the ways in which you maintain your daily health. You might be promoted, be given more responsibility, and be paid well for it. You might change jobs. However the specifics unfold, you're lucky in this area.

Consider keeping a journal about your experiences as the synchronicities occur. Or create a file on your computer or iPad. Note what types of synchronicity they are. Do they occur in clusters, with the same name, word, or phrase happening repeatedly during a relatively short period of time? Do your experiences act as guidance, confirmation, warning?

CHAPTER 8

Retrograde Planets in 2014

Every planet except the sun and moon experience retrograde motion, when the planet, as viewed from Earth, appears to be moving backward. In astrology a retrograde planet is essentially dormant, like a bear in winter. Its energy is repressed, slower, and often mixed up—as when Mercury, the planet of communication and travel, is retrograde.

During retrograde periods we tend to be less spontaneous, are prompted to think before we speak, and often backtrack through issues, situations, and relationships. We look within. The effect of a retrograde is primarily internal, even though there are many external manifestations of the retrograde.

In 2014 every planet turns retrograde, so let's take a look at when these retrogrades occur and what the effects might be for us.

Mercury

We talk quite a bit throughout the book about Mercury retrograde. It occurs three times a year, for two to three weeks. If you look at the Big Picture chapter for your sign, you'll find a lengthy discussion of Mercury retrograde and what it means for you. So here we're talking generally.

First, Mercury rules both Gemini and Virgo, so the retrogrades may have more of an impact on those two signs. When Mercury turns retrograde, your travel plans go south, there are communication snafus, you miss appointments—or discover you were never on the calendar! If you sign a contract during a Mercury retrograde, the contract may not pan out the way you hoped or the project may fall apart altogether.

In the 2000 presidential election Mercury was retrograde as the election results began to come in. Tom Brokaw announced that Al Gore had won Florida, a critical state for him, and that meant Gore had won the election. But minutes after Mercury turned direct, Brokaw said it was too early to call a winner. Ballot issues were being reported in Palm Beach County. Well, we all know where this one went—straight to the Supreme Court.

Writing now, in early 2012, it looks as if the presidential election is going to have similar issues. On November 6, the day of the election, Mercury turns retrograde in Sagittarius and doesn't turn direct again until November 26. As you read this now in late 2013 or in 2014, you already know how that election turned out!

On a personal level a Mercury retrograde impacts your life according to the sign and natal house in which it falls. Be sure to consult your natal chart as you read through the dates:

February 6 to February 28—retrograde in Pisces. Because it occurs in the early degrees of the sign, Mercury moves back into Aquarius, where it will be when Mercury turns direct again. This means that two areas of your life are affected.

June 7 to July 1—retrograde in Cancer. Again, because it occurs in the early degrees of Cancer, it moves back into Gemini, so two areas of your life are impacted.

October 4 to October 25—retrograde in Scorpio. It begins in the early degrees of Scorpio, slides back into Libra, so once again two areas of your life are affected.

Venus

Venus rules both Taurus and Libra, so they may feel the impact of a Venus retrograde more strongly than other signs. It turns retrograde once every eighteen months or so, and the retrograde period last about six weeks.

When Venus turns retrograde, your love life and finances are often impacted. Relationship issues resurface, and former lovers and spouses may suddenly appear. Friends you haven't heard from in years may get in touch out of the blue. It's an excellent time to reevaluate your closest relationships and decide what you're looking for in a partner.

If you're in a committed relationship, you and your

partner may be sifting back through issues that you thought had been resolved. One or both of you may be distant, emotionally absent, during the retrograde period.

In terms of finances your expenses may increase, and you could feel pinched. The sign and house where Venus falls during the retrograde is important, so be sure to check your natal chart. It's important to avoid buying large-ticket items. That said, however, it's possible to find great deals during a Venus retrograde. One year we bought a used car during a Venus retrograde, only to discover it had been in an accident before we'd bought it. We took it back to the company that sold us the car, and they fixed the problem. We then sold it a year later—for the same price we'd paid for it.

In 2014 Venus is retrograde between January 1 and 31 in Capricorn, a continuation of a retrograde that began in December 2013. Between January 1 and 11 Mercury is traveling with retrograde Venus, which suggests that your focus is strongly on career and professional matters, and you could be discussing things because of some rough patches.

Mars

Mars rules Aries and corules Scorpio, so these two signs may feel the impact of a Mars retrograde most strongly. A Mars retrograde occurs every two years and two months and lasts between fifty-eight to eighty-one days. In 2014 Mars begins the year retrograde in Libra, and that continues until March 1.

During a Mars retrograde your physical energy may not be up to par, so if you're partying every night, not getting enough sleep, pushing against a deadline, eating on the run . . . you may get run down. In other words, take extra good care of yourself during this period.

Mars rules our capacity for physical aggression, how we pursue our ambitions, our sexuality. The retrograde period can prompt you to bottle up anger, which can be detrimental on several levels: the anger festers and then explodes, or it festers and your blood pressure rises, or you get sick. Anger consumes enormous amounts of energy, so you end up feeling exhausted and depressed.

If you're angry at someone in particular, write the person a letter and review every word to make sure you've said exactly what you want to say. Then make a decision about whether to hold onto the letter until Mars turns direct or to give it to the person. Sometimes just writing out what you're feeling defuses the anger.

In terms of your professional life and career, projects and connections may be delayed, don't happen quickly enough, or fall apart midway through the process.

One of the best ways to deal with a Mars retrograde is through physical activity. Be sure to keep up your exercise routine. Or try new forms of exercise — yoga, pilates, brisk walking, running, or playing sports.

Jupiter

Jupiter rules Sagittarius and corules Pisces, so these two signs are apt to feel a Jupiter retrograde more strongly. Jupiter rules travel, luck, speculation, optimism, worldview, philosophy, religion, higher education, and expansion.

For about four months every year it turns retrograde. During this period you're more likely to look within for answers, and it's possible to attain a new level of awareness. You may question issues like self-worth and could be redefining yourself and your values in some way. As your worldview and spiritual beliefs expand, your external life eventually does too.

During a Jupiter retrograde meditation can be enormously beneficial. You're able to center yourself and turn within to find the answers and insights that benefit you. Take a workshop or seminar in intuitive development during the retrograde. Listen to affirmation and visualization tapes.

In 2014 there are two periods when Jupiter is retrograde. Between January 1 and March 6 it's retrograde in Cancer, a continuation of a retrograde that began in November 2013. Then on July 16 Jupiter enters Leo and turns retrograde on December 8. This retrograde lasts until April 8, 2015. Find out where Cancer and Leo fall in your natal chart; those are the areas where the retrograde will affect you most strongly.

Saturn

Saturn rules Capricorn, so when it's retrograde Capricorns are likely to feel the impact strongly. The planet turns retrograde about once a year and remains that way for about four and a half months.

Saturn rules responsibility, obligation, structure, limitations, delays, authority, conservatives, and karma. During the retrograde period everything seems to slow down. You learn how to push through self-imposed limitations because you now have the time to do so. Projects you thought were done deals may be delayed. It's wise not to try to rush things during this retrograde. Strive for what's practical and efficient.

Saturn's energy, direct or retrograde, is difficult to navigate at times. But one way or another we all manage to do so. Keep that in mind during the 2014 retrograde between January 1 and March 6, a continuation of a retrograde that began in 2013. Saturn will be retrograde in Scorpio then, so everything you encounter is likely to have an intense, bottom-line feel to it. Just try to go with the flow, and don't offer resistance!

Uranus

Uranus rules Aquarius, our individuality, sudden, unexpected change, genius, electronics, rebellion, freedom, and revolution. It turns retrograde once a year for about five months.

This planet's job is to awaken us with sudden, unexpected, and jolting events that prompt us to change the things in our lives that no longer work in our best interests. When it's retrograde, you may rebel against the status quo, whatever that is for you, and seek to free yourself from restrictive situations and relationships. You may experience sudden flashes of insight about a concern you have or that illuminates a creative endeavor in which you're involved.

Be sure to check out where Uranus is located in your natal chart. As Uranus retrogrades, you will feel it most strongly when it forms an angle to your natal Uranus or to another planet in your chart.

In 2014 Uranus in Aries is retrograde between July 21 and December 21.

Neptune

Neptune rules Pisces, higher inspiration, illusions, escapism, addiction, creativity, and spirituality. Once a year it's retrograde for about five months.

During this period your inspiration is likely to be powerful, and you'll be able to draw on deep, inner resources for any creative endeavors. Your spiritual beliefs may change or deepen, and you may spend a lot of time reading and studying about various spiritual traditions. It's an excellent period for dream work. Your dreams provide insights, information, and inspiration.

Note where Neptune is in your natal chart, and pay attention to when transiting Neptune is going to form an angle to it or to another natal planet. Neptune often blurs the boundaries between you and other people, so you may have to reestablish those boundaries.

In 2014 Neptune is retrograde in Pisces between June 9 and November 15.

Pluto

Pluto moves at a snail's pace and takes 250 years to circle the zodiac. It rules Scorpio, transformation, human evolution, and everything that is hidden and unseen. In 2014 its retrograde period is from April 14 to September 22.

During this period you have the opportunity to dive into yourself and figure out what's most important to you. Sometimes retrograde periods bring about personal loss and events that are beyond your control. That's how Pluto forces us to evolve and grow, to transform.

If you don't meditate already, start doing it before Pluto turns retrograde. That way the retrograde period may be less jarring for you, and regardless of what happens you'll remain centered and grounded.

Keep Track of Your Retrograde Experiences

During the retrograde of each of the planets this year, keep a record of what you experience. By doing this you build up knowledge about you as impacted by retrograde.

CHAPTER 9

Health Tips for 2014

Why You Take Responsibility

Statistics can be real eye openers. We recently ran across some facts related to health care in the U.S. And they are sobering.

More money per person is spent on health care in the United States than in any other country in the world. Yet life expectancy in this country ranks fiftieth, and the U.S. lags behind other wealthy nations in infant mortality. According to the Institute of Medicine, the United States is the only country in the world that doesn't ensure that all its citizens have health coverage.

When Obama signed the Affordable Care Act into law in 2010, the politically conservative faction screamed that it was socialism. It's not. Socialized medicine is full coverage by the *government*. The mandate in the U.S. was a triumph for private insurance companies, whose bottom line is profit, not health. They will now gain nearly 50 million new clients.

In all fairness, there are some good things about this mandate. Children can be on their parents' insurance policies until the age of twenty-six, and no one can be denied health insurance because of a preexisting condition. Not surprisingly, the mandate has been challenged in court and will come before the Supreme Court in March 2011. You, reading this in 2014, already know the outcome. We don't.

One of the most famous moments in the health care debacle was when an older woman at a Tea Party meeting waved her sign—*No to Obama Care*—while she shouted, "Keep your hands off my Medicare!"

You know, Medicare, the *government-run* insurance program for people sixty-five and older. Medicare for all should have been implemented, not mandated by health insurance.

Until insurance companies are removed from health care, the health care in this country will continue to be a discriminatory system. The real death panels will continue to be insurance companies who deny care for profit.

If nothing else, that debate and the reality of health care in this country should encourage you to take charge of your own health. Here are some simple suggestions:

1) *If you don't have a regular exercise routine yet, start one.* Pick something that you know you can do daily.

2) *Watch what you eat. Read the labels on the food you buy.* How much sodium is there in your favorite foods? How much cholesterol? Fats? Even organic foods have a high sodium content. The other day at Whole Foods we picked up some soy bacon and then

turned the box over to look at the contents. For a single slice of soy bacon, the nutritional facts state:

Total fat—1 gram
No saturated or trans fat, no polyunsaturated or monounsaturated fats
Cholesterol—0 mg
Sodium—140 mg
Potassium—40 mg
No carbs, no sugar
Protein—2 g

That's a lot of sodium for a single skinny slice of soy bacon! Compare this to our favorite organic chicken sausage, however, which has 460 mg of sodium for a single link, and the soy bacon looks good. Once you get into the habit of reading the labels, you will be more careful in your selection of foods.

3) *Meditation and yoga are two healthy practices you might consider*. Meditation has been shown to: lower blood pressure and oxygen consumption, decrease respiratory rate, slow heart rate, reduce anxiety and stress, and enhance the immune system. Yoga increases your physical flexibility—and eventually your emotional and mental flexibility as well. It helps to strengthen your body, improves muscle tone, improves posture, improves lung capacity because of the deep breathing involved, and reduces stress.

4) *Try various nutritional and vitamin programs*. Educate yourself. The Internet is filled with health and fitness Web sites.

5) *Try a homeopathic practitioner or acupuncturist before you run to your doctor for a prescription*.

If you were an alien watching the evening news and the drug commercials that sponsor it, you might get the impression that Americans are a sickly lot in search of the quickest fix. While drugs certainly have their place, more and more Americans are seeking alternative treatments for whatever ails them. From acupuncture to yoga and homeopathy, from vitamin regimens to nutritional programs, more of us are taking control over our own health and bodies.

6) *Take inventory of your beliefs*. If medical intuitives like Louise Hay, Carolyn Myss, and Mona Lisa Schultz are correct, our health is about more than just eating right and getting sufficient exercise. It's also about our emotions, inner worlds, and belief systems. How happy are you in your job? Your closest partnerships? Your friendships? Are you generally happy with the money you earn? What would you change about your life? Do you believe you have free will or that everything is destined? Is your mood generally upbeat? Do you feel you have choices? Do you feel empowered? By asking yourself these kinds of questions, you can glean a sense of your emotional state at any given time. And the state of your emotions may tell you a great deal about the state of your health.

7) *Forgive yourself and others.* Resentment that you keep bottled up inside you for months or even years can adversely affect your health. It's why medical intuitives and holistic physicians recommend practicing the art of forgiveness. It's not easy to forgive people who have hurt you, but once you're able to forgive them, you're releasing resentment.

8) *Practice the art of appreciation. Expect the best from others.* If you can get into the habit of doing

these two things, you're well ahead of the game in maintaining your health.

The Physical You

These descriptions fit both sun and rising signs. For a more complete look at the physical you, of course, your entire natal chart should be taken into account, with a particularly close look at the sign of your moon—the root of your emotions, the cradle of your inner world.

Aries

Rules: Head and Face

2014 Tip:

In this year of the new you try something new in the way you care for yourself and your health.

Health and Fitness

Aries rules the head and face, so these areas are often the most vulnerable physically. Headaches, dizziness, and skin eruptions can be common. If you're an athletic Aries, do more of whatever it is that you enjoy. Competitive sports? Great, go for it. Long distance runner? Run farther. Gym? Double your time and your workout. Yoga once a week? Do it three times a week. One way or another, you need to burn off your excessive energy so that it doesn't turn inward and short-circuit your body!

As a cardinal fire sign, you're an active person who gravitates toward daring, risky sports—mountain climbing, rappelling, bungee jumping, trekking through high mountainous regions, leaping out of airplanes. It's probably a great idea to have good health insurance or to have a Louise Hay attitude toward your health—*I'm attracting only magnificent experiences into my life.*

For maximum benefit, you probably should try to eliminate red meat from your diet. Chicken and fish are fine, but a vegan diet would be best. Herbs like mustard, eye-bright, and bay are beneficial for you. Any antioxidant is helpful—particularly vitamins C, E, A, or Lutein for your eyes, zinc, Co-Q10, Black Cohosh if you're a female in menopause, or Saw Palmetto if you're a man older than fifty. If you pull a muscle or throw your back out of whack, look for a good acupuncturist and avoid pain killers.

In this year of the new you, practice what you learned last year to transform yourself from the inside out. Start with your thoughts. Notice what you think throughout a given day. If you notice that a lot of negative thoughts surface, nudge them on their way by reaching for more positive ones.

Taurus

Rules: Neck, Throat, Cervical Vertebrae

2014 Tip:

In this year of the new you, reach out to strangers, join a group of like-minded individuals, and keep expressing your feelings. Blogging is one excellent way to do that.

Health and Fitness

Thanks to the sensuality of your sign, you may be a gourmet cook and enjoy rich foods. But because your metabolism may be somewhat slow, you benefit from daily exercise and moderation in your diet. In fact, moderation in all things is probably a good rule to follow.

As a fixed earth sign, you benefit from any outdoor activity, and the more physical it is, the better it is for you. Hiking, skiing, windsurfing, biking are all excellent pursuits. You also benefit from any mind/body discipline like tai chi or yoga. The latter is especially good since it keeps you flexible, and that flexibility spills over into your attitudes and beliefs and the way you deal with situations and people. You probably enjoy puttering in a garden, but because you have such an artistic side, you don't just putter. You remake the garden into a work of art—fountains, bold colors, mysterious paths that twist through greenery and flowers. Once you add wind chimes and bird feeders, nature's music adds the finishing touches.

If your job entails long hours of sitting in front of a computer, your neck and shoulders may be more tense than usual. You would benefit through regular massage and hot tub soaks.

If you're the silent type of Taurus, then chances are you don't discuss your emotions. This tendency can cause health challenges if you keep anger or resentment bottled up inside you. Best to have an outlet—through exercise, for example, or through some sort of creative endeavor. Art, music, photography, writing—

any of those would help. Better yet, learn to open up with at least one or two people!

Gemini

Rules: Hands, Arms, Lungs, Nervous System

2014 Tip:

In this year of the new you, practice focusing on one thing at a time. Don't spread yourself too thinly.

Health and Fitness

You benefit from periodic breaks in your established routine. Whether it's a trip to some exotic port or a trip to the grocery, it's a breath of fresh air, a way to hit the pause button on your busy mind. Regular physical exercise helps to bleed off some of your energy and keeps your already youthful body supple and in shape.

As a mutable air sign, you need intellectual stimulation and a constant array of experiences and information to keep your curiosity piqued. Otherwise it's too easy for all that nervous energy to turn inward and affect your health. The kind of work you do is important in the overall scheme of your health. You do best in nonroutine kinds of work with flexible hours or, preferably, in a profession where you make your own hours! Any job in communication, travel, public relations, would suit you. When you're passionate about what you do, you're happier. If you're happy, your immune system remains healthy.

With your natural dexterity and coordination, you

would do well at yoga. If you don't take classes yet, sign up for some. Not only will they keep you flexible, but you'll benefit mentally. Meditation would also be an excellent practice for you. Anything to calm your busy head!

Since your respiratory and nervous systems are your most vulnerable areas, your diet should include plenty of fish, fresh fruits, and vegetables. If you live in a place where you can garden, then plant some of these items in a garden for optimum freshness. Vitamin C, zinc, the B vitamins, and vitamins E and A are also beneficial for you. With your energy always in fast-forward, it's smart to get at least seven and preferably eight hours of sleep a night. If you're the type of Gemini with a high metabolism, you benefit from eating several small meals throughout the day rather than just the usual three.

Cancer

Rules: Breasts, Stomach, Digestive System

2014 Tip:

During this year of the new you, practice being more objective.

Health and Fitness

As a cardinal water sign, you benefit from proximity to water. If you can live or work close to a body of water, you'll notice a marked difference in your energy and intuition and how you feel and think. Even a vacation close to it is healing. This seems to hold true not only for Cancer sun signs, but for moon and rising signs in Cancer too. The body of water can be anything—a lake, river, ocean, salt marsh, even a pond!

Not surprisingly, you benefit from any kind of water sport, even a day at the beach or a picnic by the river. The point is that water speaks to you. It feels like your natural element. You might want to read *The Secret of Water* or any of the other books by Masaru Emoto. You will never think of water in the same way again and will be more conscious of how human emotions affect water—and thus our bodies, since we consist of nearly 70 percent water.

Emotionally you may cling to past injuries and hurts more than other signs or may still be dragging around issues from childhood or even from a past life. Unresolved emotional stuff can lodge in your body and create problems. So it's important that you rid yourself of past resentments and anger. Use hypnosis to dislodge these feelings. Forgive and forget. Have a past-life regression. Read Louise Hay's book *You Can Heal Your Life.*

If you have a moon, rising, or another planet in an earth sign, consider regular workouts at a gym.

Leo

Rules: Heart, Back, Spinal Cord

2014 Tip:

In this year of the new you, keep drama to a minimum. Whenever you feel yourself at the brink of an emotional outburst or meltdown, detach, step back.

Health and Fitness

Leo rules the heart. So you benefit from a low-fat diet, exercise, work that you love, and relationships in which you are recognized as the unique person that you are. Yes, those last two things count in the overall picture of your health!

Let's talk about your work. Acting, of course, is what you're known for. And performance. And politics. And, well, anything where you can show off your abundant talents. So if right now you're locked into a humdrum job, low person on the bureaucratic totem pole, and don't receive the attention you feel you deserve, then your pride and ambition are suffering. That, in turn, creates resentment that could be eating you alive. Turn the situation around by finding a career or an outlet where your talents shine and you're appreciated and recognized. You're a natural leader whose flamboyant style and magnetism attract the supporters who can help you.

You have a temper, but once you blow, that's it. Unlike Cancer, you don't hold on to grudges or harbor resentments or anger from childhood. You tend to be forward looking in your outlook, and your natural optimism is healthy for your heart and immune system. Anything you can do to maintain your cheerful disposition is a plus. When you feel yourself getting down, rent comedies, find books that make you laugh out loud, blog about your feelings.

Virgo

Rules: Intestines, Abdomen, Female Reproductive System

2014 Tip:

Since this is the year of the new you, stick to your exercise routine. Do it regularly. And strive not to be self-critical.

Health and Fitness

If you're the type of Virgo who worries and frets a lot, the first place it's likely to show up is in your digestive tract. You might have had colic as an infant, stomach upsets as a teenager, ulcers as an adult. The best way to mitigate this tendency, of course, is to learn how NOT to worry and to simply go with the flow.

You do best on a diet that includes plenty of fresh fruits and vegetables, fish, and chicken. Try to stay away from fried or heavily spiced foods. Red meat might be difficult to digest. If you live in a place where fresh fruits and vegetables are difficult to find during the winter, supplement your diet with the appropriate vitamins and minerals. If you're a fussy eater—and some Virgos are—the vitamin and mineral supplements are even more important.

You benefit from hot baths, massages, anything that allows you to relax into the moment. Yoga, running, swimming, gym workouts—any of these exercise regimens benefit you. Some Virgos, particularly double Virgos—with a moon or rising in that sign—have an acute sense of smell. If you're one of those, be sure to treat yourself to scented soaps and lotions, fragrant candles and incense, and any other scent that soothes your soul.

Virgo is typically associated with service, and you may find that whenever you do a good deed for someone, when you volunteer your time or expertise, you feel better about yourself and life in general. The more you can do to trigger these feelings, the healthier you'll be. You have a tendency toward self-criticism that's part and parcel of your need for perfection, and whenever you find yourself shifting into that critical frame of mind, stop it in its tracks. Reach for a more uplifting thought. This will help you to maintain your health.

Libra

Rules: Lower Back, Kidney, Diaphragm

2014 Tip:

During this year of the new you, try not to bend over backward to please the people in your life.

Health and Fitness

If your love life is terrific, then your health probably is too. You're happiest when you're in a relationship, preferably a committed, lifetime relationship. When things between you and your partner are on an even keel, your energy is greater, your immune system works without a hitch, you sleep more soundly, and you're more apt to have a healthier lifestyle.

You prefer working in an environment that's aesthetically pleasing, where there's a minimum of drama, and with congenial people. If your work situation doesn't fit that description, it could affect your health—and for the same reason as a love life that is lacking—emotions. Your lower back, kidneys, and diaphragm are vulnerable areas for you and unvented emotions could manifest in those areas first. If it isn't possible to change jobs or careers right now, then find an artistic outlet for your creative expression. Music, photography, art, writing, dance, any area that allows you to flex your creativity.

You benefit from yoga, walking, swimming, and any kind of exercise that strengthen your lower back muscles. Meditation is also beneficial, particularly when it's combined with an awareness of breathing.

The healthiest diet for you should consist of foods with varied tastes, plenty of fresh fruits and vegetables, organic if possible, and a minimum of meats. Anything that benefits your kidneys is good. Drink at least eight glasses of water a day, so that your kidneys are continually flushed out.

Scorpio

Rules: Sexual Organs, Elimination

2014 Tip:

In this year of the new you, listen closely to your intuition, particularly in health matters.

Health and Fitness

As a fixed water sign, you probably benefit by a proximity to water every bit as much as Cancer does. Lake, ocean, river, ocean, pond, salt marsh—take your pick. If none of these is available, put a fountain in your backyard or somewhere in your house, and create a meditation area. It's important that you have a quiet center where you can decompress at the end of the day, particularly if you have a busy family life and a lot of demands on your time.

You tend to keep a lot of emotion locked inside, and if the emotions are negative—resentment, anger—they fester and affect your health. So try to find someone you can talk to freely about your emotions—a partner, friend, family member. Or pour these feelings into a creative outlet. One way or another, get them out.

Scorpio rules the sexual and elimination organs, so these areas could be where ill health hits first. Be sure that you eat plenty of roughage in your diet and enjoy what you eat, while you're eating it. Stay away from the usual culprits—fried or heavily processed foods. You do best with plenty of fresh food, but may want to consider eliminating red meats. Consider colonic treatments for cleaning out the bowels.

For your overall health, it's important to enjoy sex with a partner whom you trust. Avoid using sex as a leverage for power in a relationship.

Sagittarius

Rules: Hips, Thighs, Liver

2014 Tip:

The new you in 2014 is a person who commits to a healthy lifestyle.

Health and Fitness

As a mutable fire sign, you can't tolerate any kind of restriction or limitation on your freedom. You must be able to get up and go whenever you want. If you work in a job that demands you punch a time clock, where your hours are strictly regulated, or are in a relationship where you feel constricted, you probably aren't happy. For a naturally buoyant and happy person like you, that could spell health challenges. Sadge rules the hips, the sacral region of the spine, the coccygeal vertebrae, the femur, the ileum, the iliac arteries, and the sciatic nerves, so any of these areas could be impacted health-wise.

You benefit from any kind of athletic activity. From competitive sports to an exercise regimen you create, your body craves regular activity. You also benefit from yoga, which keeps your spine and hips flexible.

If you're prone to putting on weight—and even if you're not!—strive to minimize sweets and carbs in your diet. The usual recommendations—abundant fresh vegetables and fruits—also apply. If you're the type who eats on the run, you may be eating fast or heavily processed foods and should try to keep that to a minimum or eliminate it altogether. Even though your digestive system is hardy enough to tolerate just about anything, the fast foods and processed foods add carbs and calories.

Antioxidants are beneficial, of course, and these include vitamins C, A, and E. Minerals like zinc should be included in your diet and also a glucosamine supplement for joints.

Capricorn

Rules: Knees, Skin, Bones

2014 Tip:

The new you understands the value of relaxation and doing what you enjoy.

Health and Fitness

Since you seem to have been born with an innate sense of where you're going—or want to go—it's likely that you take care of yourself. You know the routine as well as anyone—eat right, stay fit, exercise, get enough rest. But there are other components to living long and prospering (to paraphrase Spock!). And that's your emotions.

You, like Scorpio, are secretive, although your motives are different. For you it's a privacy factor more than anything else. You keep your emotions to yourself and may not express what you feel when you feel it. This can create blockages in your body, notably in your joints or knees. It's vital that you learn to vent your emotions, to rid yourself of anger before it has a chance to move inward.

You're focused, ambitious, and patient in the attainment of your goals. But your work—your satisfaction with it—is a primary component in your health. If you feel you've reached a dead end in your career, if you're frustrated more often than you're happy with what you do, it's time to revamp and get out of Dodge. By taking clear, definite steps toward something else, you feel you're more in control of your destiny and mitigate the possibility of health challenges.

Since your knees are vulnerable, running is probably not the best form of exercise for you, unless you do it only once or twice a week and engage in some other form of exercise the rest of the time. For a cardio workout that isn't as tough on your knees, try a rowing machine. For general flexibility, there's nothing like yoga!

Aquarius

Rules: Ankles, Shins, Circulatory System

2014 Tip:

In this year of the new you, Aquarius, you maintain your exercise routine. No more cheating!

Health and Fitness

Let's start with the effect of Uranus ruling your sign. It sometimes can set your nerves on edge—too many sounds, too much chaos around you, loud noises deep into the night, the backfiring of cars, the incessant drone of traffic, even a crowd at the local mall. You're sensitive to all of that. It's part of what makes it important for you to have a private space to which you can withdraw—a quiet back yard filled with plants, a room inside your house with an altar for your Wiccan practice, filled with scents from candles or incense that soothe your frazzled nerves. Or perhaps a book on tape can shut it all out. But shut it out you must to protect your health.

Because you live so much inside your own head, exercise is definitely beneficial for you. It doesn't have to be anything complicated—yoga done in the privacy of your own home, long walks, regular bike rides. But do *something* to ground your body, to get your blood moving, to silence the buzz inside your head. It will all benefit your health.

Nutrition? Well for an Aquarian this can go any number of different ways. You enjoy different types of food, so that's a place to start—with what you *enjoy*. The foods are likely to be unusual—organically grown, for instance, prepared in unusual ways, or purchased from a local co-op. If you live in the city, perhaps you purchase food from a grocery store you've been frequenting for years. The idea here is that *you* know what's best for your body, what you can tolerate, what you need. Even though Aquarians aren't generally as in touch with their bodies as earth signs, they have an intuitive sense about what works for them. In the end that's all that matters.

Pisces

Rules: Feet, Lymphatic System

2014 Tip:

The new you treats yourself as you treat others.

Health and Fitness

Let's start with emotions. Let's start with the fact that you're a psychic sponge, able to absorb other people's moods and thoughts with the ease of a magnet attracting every other piece of metal around it. Yes, let's start there. It's why you should associate only with optimis-

tic, upbeat people. The negative types steal your energy, wreck your immune system, and leave you in a tearful mess at the end of the rainbow with nothing to show for your journey.

Like your fellow water signs Cancer and Scorpio, you probably benefit from proximity to water. Whether you live near water, work near it, or vacation near it, water refreshes your soul, spirit, intuition, and immune system. Read Masaru Emoto's books on how water responds to emotions and intent. You'll never think about water in the same way again. You'll never think about your sun sign in the same way again either.

You benefit from any kind of exercise, but try something that speaks to your soul. Swimming. Rowing, but in an actual boat, on an actual river instead of in a gym. Even a hot tub where you kick your legs is beneficial. Pay attention to the water you drink. Is your tap water filled with fluorides? Then avoid it, and look for distilled water. Drink at least eight glasses a day. Indulge yourself in massages, foot reflexology, periodic dips in the ocean. Any ocean.

CHAPTER 10

Your Creativity in 2014

We're innately creative beings who reinvent ourselves constantly. From our appearances to the way we work to our interactions with others, we rarely repeat the same action in exactly the same way. In 2014 it's important that we use our creativity to solve problems and meet challenges in our work, careers, and relationships.

Due to rapidly changing technology, some of us may need to reinvent ourselves professionally. With the popularity of ebooks, for instance, the publishing industry is no longer as centralized as it once was. Writers can now self-publish through any number of services and link their books to Amazon. Artists or photographers who once had to haul around portfolios can now have digital portfolios. Actors and actresses who once had to carry around scripts while learning their lines can now use iPads to view their lines.

How can you use your creativity to redefine yourself this year? Let's take a look.

Aries

As a natural trailblazer and entrepreneur, you have no trouble coming up with new ideas about how to reinvent yourself. Your challenge, though, is carrying through from beginning to end.

The carry-through may be easier for you to accomplish while Jupiter is in fellow fire sign Leo, between July 16, 2014, and August 11, 2015. Jupiter helps you to expand your ideas, to develop your creativity to the point where it becomes second nature. You also have Uranus in your sign helping you to get rid of whatever has gone stale in your life.

So during 2014 don't hesitate to think outside the box, take professional and emotional risks, and follow impulses. It's your path to embracing change.

Taurus

As a fixed earth sign, you are slow to change. You tend to hold on to clothes you no longer wear, jobs that don't suit you, relationships that you've outgrown. In any area where you feel dissatisfaction this year, take a closer look and try to determine if your feelings are transitory, just a mood, or whether it's something more than that. If your dissatisfaction is genuine, how can you change things around?

If your job is the problem, perhaps there are additional skills you can learn and credentials you can garner that will enable you to land a better job that is more suited to your temperament and in a field you love. That's the point here: change that you enjoy, that helps you to evolve creatively.

Develop a strategy, and then use your resoluteness to make it work. This process will be easier for you between January 1 and July 16, while Jupiter transits compatible water sign Cancer and expands your intuition.

Gemini

Change is your middle name. Your challenge, though, is that you sometimes change so rapidly that you aren't sure who you are when you get up in the morning. It's why your sign depicts twins!

In 2014 use your adaptability and innate creativity to focus on one particular area in your life that you would like to change—job, career, relationships, finances. Whatever the area is, decide what you want, how you might best attain it, and then pursue it. If you're the kind of Gemini who enjoys writing, consider blogging about your experiences. You never know how it may help or influence someone else.

Your best time for initiating change and using your creativity to bring it about falls between July 16, 2014, and August 11, 2015, when Jupiter transits compatible fire sign Leo. During this period you're on a creative roll.

Cancer

You're usually so in touch with your feelings that you know when dissatisfaction is just a passing mood and when it addresses something deeper. So take that area of your life where you're feeling genuine dissatisfaction and try to see it objectively. That may be a challenge for you, Cancer. You tend to view the world through a subjective lens, but in this instance objectivity will serve you better.

Once you've identified whatever it is you want to change, use your prodigious intuition to figure out how to initiate the change. Use dream recall, meditation, visualization, and the other intuitive tools you possess. Then act on that information, trusting that your guidance will bring about what you desire.

Synchronicities may proliferate during this process, so be sure to decipher the messages, these signs and symbols that lead you through the unknown. This process will be greatly facilitated between January 1 and July 16, when Jupiter transits your sign.

Leo

Like your fixed-sign cousin Taurus, you're not crazy about change. You like things the way they are, thank you very much. Yet when you feel a deep dissatisfaction about something in your life, you certainly have the creative abilities to initiate change and transform your job, relationships, finances, whatever it is.

As Jupiter transits your sign between July 16, 2014, and August 11, 2015, there will be a lot of changes. This planet seeks to expand your life and creative abilities and ushers in the opportunities for doing so. Your challenge will be to avoid drama and just get on with it.

Jupiter's transit through Cancer from January 1 to July 16 will enable you to hone in on beliefs and attitudes that may be holding you back. Once you understand the origin of these beliefs, you can use them as creative fodder, so they are really illuminated to your conscious mind, and change them. Then you can change those beliefs, and your life will change accordingly.

Virgo

You, like your mutable cousin Gemini, welcome change. But you prefer it to occur on your terms, in your time frame, according to your specifications; in other words, when you're ready for it. But because you share the planet with seven billion other souls, change often happens on its own, and then you have to adapt quickly to the new circumstances. You have a plethora of creative talents that enable you to do this.

Your creativity, in fact, is central to who you are. Whether change is something you initiate, or it comes about due to global events, your creativity kicks in, and you're able to move with the flow. Your creativity is apt to be enormously powerful between January 1 and July 15, when Jupiter transits compatible water sign Cancer.

During this transit your intuition expands, and you're able to tap deep creative reservoirs in your being. Don't fritter away this opportunity for personal and professional growth.

Libra

You, like your cardinal cousins Aries and Cancer, are a focused individual and aren't fond of change that is thrust upon you. But when that happens, your creative talents rush in to help you sort things out, and you're able to use the change to your advantage.

If there's some area of your life where you feel dissatisfied, bring your enormous focus to bear on changing it. Don't concentrate on what's wrong, but on the end result you want. See it vividly in your mind—a new you, more money, a better job, a relationship. Whatever it is, imagine it and back that image with emotion.

Your best time for making things happen occurs during Jupiter's transit of compatible fire sign Leo between July 16, 2014, and August 11, 2015.

Scorpio

Your creativity is legendary among the people who know you, and in 2014 it could become legendary to the rest of the world too. You, like your fixed cousins Taurus and Leo, tend to be quite stubborn about how to do something. In 2014 this stubbornness serves you well when it comes to your creative endeavors. You know for an end product, so stick to what you know. However, be open to suggestions by other creative people.

If there are areas of your life that beg for change, shed the stubbornness, delve deeply into your intuitive ability, and figure out what your ideal is. Then listen to your intuition about how to attract the ideal into your life.

This process will be easier when Jupiter is in fellow water sign Cancer between January 1 and July 16.

Sagittarius

You enjoy change, as long as it doesn't restrict your freedom. After all, the source of your creativity is that very freedom you savor, which is as necessary to your life as oxygen.

If there is a particular area of your life that dissatisfies you, it's time to hit the road, Sadge, and allow your creativity to come up with options, solutions, answers, a strategy. Your muse will come out of hiding as soon as you're traveling, and then it's up to you to listen closely, interpret, and create.

Your best time for engaging this process is when Jupiter transits fellow fire sign Leo between July 16, 2014, and August 11, 2015.

Capricorn

You're a focused, self-directed individual who wants life to be grounded, tangible, and unfold one step at a time. You usually know when something in your life is *off,* but may not know how to correct it. That's when your creativity sweeps in and discovers the options, solutions, the new path.

During Jupiter's transit of Cancer, your opposite sign, between January 1 and July 16 your intuition deepens and becomes one of your staunchest allies. A family member or partner—business or romantic—may prove helpful in changing something essential in your life.

The beauty of Capricorn's energy is simple. You steadily climb the mountain toward your goal, and when you encounter a block, you search for and usually find an alternate path to wherever you're going.

Aquarius

You and your fixed-sign cousins—Taurus, Leo, Scorpio—aren't fond of change. But you understand that change is inevitable, that it's the only constant, and so you embrace it as you do most things in life, with your intellect. Once you grasp the core of what's happening, you allow yourself to feel your way through it.

You're a visionary, and your creativity reflects that. You're able to spot a trend long before it reaches a tipping point and use that knowledge and foresight to transform any area of your life with which you're dissatisfied. The best time to tackle this process is when Jupiter transits Leo, your opposite sign, between July 16, 2014, and August 11, 2015.

During this period your business and personal partnerships expand, you have a chance to demonstrate your creative abilities, and a partner is instrumental in helping you to create a life that suits you in every way.

Pisces

You and your mutable cousins—Gemini, Virgo, and Sagittarius—are best equipped to deal with change. But for you any kind of change requires an emotional adjustment, and this is where things can get dicey.

You are in touch with your emotions, so you know when something is off kilter. But you may not know how to change whatever it is. This is when your powerful imagination comes into play. Whatever you can imagine and back with emotion can be brought into your life. Allow your creativity to explore your options. Be innovative.

For you Jupiter's transit through fellow water sign Cancer will be the best time to experiment. The dates: January 1 to July 16.

CHAPTER 11

Aspects

An aspect is the angle that planets make to other planets in a natal chart—by transit, progression, solar return, or any other system in astrology. For the purpose of this book, we primarily look at where these transiting planets hit your solar houses and the angles they make to your sun and each other. Some of these angles are beneficial, others are challenging. Think of aspects as a symbolic network of arteries and veins that transports the blood of astrology. In a natal chart these angles connect our inner and outer worlds, accentuate certain traits, and play down others. Each aspect represents a certain type of energy, so there really aren't any good or bad aspects because energy is neutral. It's what we do with the energy that counts. It comes back to free will. When transiting planets make angles to each other and to our natal planets, energy is also exchanged.

For instance, every year there is at least one very lucky day when the transiting sun and transiting Jupiter form a beneficial angle to each other—a conjunction (same sign and degree), a sextile (60 degrees apart), or a trine (120 degrees apart). In 2014 there are two such dates—July 25–26, when the sun and Jupiter are conjunct. This means that the sun's life energy and Jupiter's expansive energy combine and create, well, some magic for all of us! It's especially good for Leo and other fire signs. But since we all have Leo somewhere in our charts, these two days are lucky for the rest of us too.

If you look back to the presidential election in November 2008, Saturn in Virgo and Uranus in Pisces formed an exact opposition to each other. They were 180 degrees apart, an aspect that is like a tug-of-war. In this case the tug-of-war was between the candidate that represented the old paradigm, the established order—Saturn—and the candidate who symbolized sweeping change—Uranus.

Aspects are most powerful as they are approaching exactness. So even though a conjunction, for example, is 00 degrees of separation or a square is technically 90 degrees of separation, many astrologers use *orbs* that can be as wide as 5 or 10 degrees. Some astrologers use small orbs, but others assign larger orbs for the sun and moon and smaller orbs for other planets. The closer the orb, the more powerful the combination. If you're sensitive to transits, then, you may be feeling lucky for several days before and after July 25–26.

In terms of a natal chart, any transiting planet that is approaching an aspect with one of your natal planets is also most powerful on its approach. The traditional aspects have been used since the second century A.D. They are the conjunction, sextile, square, trine, and opposition. These aspects are considered to be the major or hard angles and are also the most powerful. There are other minor aspects that astrologers use, but for the purpose of this chapter, we'll only talk about the traditional aspects.

Conjunction, Major Hard Aspect, 0 Degrees

This aspect is easy to identify—clusters of planets within a few degrees of each other, usually but not always in the same sign and house. But it's a complex aspect because energies combine, fuse, merge. Think of it as power and intensity, and that's true whether it's in your natal chart or is a transiting planet conjuncting your sun sign. If you have conjunctions in your natal chart, the astrologer who reads for you should address what it means and how you can use it to maximize your potential.

Sextile, Major Soft Aspect, 60 Degrees

Planets that are sextile to each other flow well together, feed each other. According to house and sign, they may confer artistic ability, the gift of gab, greater imagination, higher intuition.

Square, Major Hard Aspect, 90 Degrees

Friction, angst, *oh my God, the sky is falling*: that's how squares feel in a natal chart. The sky, of course, is never falling, but the friction and angst are quite real and act as triggers for action and forward thrust. They force us to develop, evolve, and reach aggressively for our desires.

Trines, Major Soft Aspect, 120 Degrees

This aspect works like a sextile, linking energies in a harmonious way. It's associated with general ease and good fortune, and it means the same whether it's in the natal chart or by transit. People with a lot of trines in their natural charts are sometimes at a disadvantage because things come so easily to them.

Opposition, Major Hard Aspect, 180 Degrees

This aspect feels like a persistent itch that you can't reach and usually involves polarities—Taurus/Scorpio, for example, or Aries/Libra. It brings about change through conflict and sometimes represents traits we project onto others because we haven't fully integrated them into ourselves. Again the opposition applies to transits as well as to natal planets.

When checking the transits in your own chart, always keep in mind the meanings of the two planets involved, the meanings of the houses, and the meanings of the aspects.

Some other minor aspects that astrologers use are:

- the semi-square, 45 degrees. It creates irritation and friction between the planets involved.
- the septile, 51 degrees. Indicative of harmony and union in a nontraditional way. Can suggest spiritual power.
- the quincunx or inconjunct, 150 degrees separation. Indicates a need for adjustment in attitude and beliefs.

CHAPTER 12

The Astrological Neighborhood

Several years ago a Google search for the word *astrology* turned up about 40 million links. Today a Google search results in 114 million links. It suggests that as greater numbers of people search for information and insights, astrology has exploded in popularity.

You can find sites for virtually any aspect of this fascinating field, but some sites are far superior and more user friendly than others. These sites offer free natal charts, daily transits, monthly horoscopes, and political and world predictions. It's all at your fingertips. We have a blog at www.sydneyomarr.blogspot .com. In addition, here are some great astrology sites:

www.astrologyzone.com: Susan Miller's site is a favorite for neophytes and pros alike. Every month she writes about several words per sign, with detailed predictions for the month. She cites the best days for romance, finances, and career matters. She discusses new and full moons, eclipses, and their impact on your sun sign, and provides information on various aspects that are coming up in a given month. You can also obtain a free natal chart. Her site is chocked with information and is user friendly, and her predictions are eerily accurate.

www.astro.com: This site is also jammed with information. Here you can get a free natal chart, see immediately where the planets are today, use the ephemeris, and find out the geographical coordinates for a particular city. There are other interesting tidbits as well—celebrities born on a given day and fascinating and informative articles by some of the world's best astrologers. This site is perfect for the beginner, the intermediary, and the advanced astrologer.

www.moonvalleyastrologer.com: Celeste Teal is *the* expert on eclipses, a specialized area of astrology that few have researched the way she has. Her two books on eclipses are seminal works. She also provides informative articles on various aspects of astrology. If you're new to astrology, there's plenty on this site to whet your appetite. Regardless of your expertise in astrology, Celeste's site offers information for everyone.

www.astrocollege.com: Lois Rodden's site is extraordinary. This woman spent most of her life collecting birth data and then created a piece of software that is invaluable in research. For example, you can compare charts of individuals in virtually any field and discover what astrological components they have in common. Let's say you're looking for artists who all had Leo suns, Capricorn moons, and Scorpio rising. You enter those criteria, and the software delivers names. The software also provides *signatures*—a certain combination of aspects and other factors that points to particular characteristics in an individual. In addition, the site rates and sells astrology software. Lois has passed on, but her work survives.

http://astrofuturetrends.com: Author and astrologer Anthony Louis does just what the site says. He predicts future trends, covers political stuff, and provides an overall view of astrology.

www.starlightnews.com: Click on *Nancy's blog.* Here you'll find the latest predictions and insights about world affairs. Nancy's predictions about politics have been right on. Before the 2004 election she made some predictions about tight senatorial races that were totally accurate. She also called the presidential race in 2008. Since we're writing this in early 2012, we don't know yet what her predictions are for 2012, but she'll undoubtedly prove to be accurate. She receives hundreds of comments for her posts, and some of them are as informative as her posts.

www.synchrosecrets.com/synchrosecrets: About synchronicities—what they are, how they show up in our lives, what they might mean, and hundreds of stories. There are occasional posts on astrological factors— like Mercury retrogrades!

Software

In the days before computers a natal chart or anything else connected to astrology had to be configured manually, through complicated mathematical formulae that left you gasping. Astrology software has truly transformed the study of astrology and our knowledge about it. Since the late 1980s, when we began using astrology software, the choices have multiplied.

Our first piece of software was a really simply program we found at a computer store for ten bucks. It erected a chart in about sixty seconds. There it was, rising, moon, sun, planets, the houses, everything set up on the computer screen as if by magic. In the late 1990s we bought our first really terrific astrology software from Matrix for about $300. In the years since, **http://www.astrologysoftware.com** has supplied us with endless data and information and revolutionized the study of astrology.

But it's not just enough to have a great piece of software. When your computer crashes, when you receive updates that screw up, when Windows updates to a new system, you call the Matrix help line and their people walk you through it until everything works. And the employees on their help lines aren't outsourced. You won't reach India. You'll talk to someone in Michigan who is not only an astrologer, but a computer geek who knows how to fix your problem. And if by some fluke they can't fix your problem, they'll credit you for one of their other terrific programs.

The only complaint we have about Matrix is that to activate the software, you have to call or contact them through the Internet to receive a special code. If your computer crashes, if you buy a new PC or laptop . . . well, it's annoying. When you pay this much for software, you shouldn't have to obtain a special access code.

Another great piece of software is SolarFire. Astrologers are as dedicated to this program as they are to Matrix's software. Check out http://www.alabe.com for current prices. While the two programs offer similar features and capabilities, preferences seem to be individual. Both Matrix's Winstar and astrolabe's SolarFire offer many of the same features—natal charts, transits, progressed charts, solar chart, and interpretations. They both feature material about fixed stars, aspects, lunations, eclipses, and all the other important components you could possibly want or need. The main difference lies in the appearance of the charts and how the information is presented.

Kepler's astrology program—http://www.astrosoftware.com—is beautiful in its rendition of charts, interpretations, and just about anything any astrologer could use or need. We like it for its ease, its beauty. But it lacks the complexity of both Winstar and Solar-Fire. The program simply doesn't do as much.

If your exploration of astrology takes you deeper, there are other software programs that take you there. Bernadette Brady is the undisputed mistress of fixed stars. Her software program, Starlight, is remarkable not only for its accuracy, but for its presentation. You will never think of fixed stars in the same way once you play with this program. What won't make sense in a natal chart interpretation suddenly snaps into clarity when you use her software. Be sure to download a print to file version for the software—through a PDF file—so that you can maximize usage. Their website: http://www.zyntara.com.

Lois Rodden's AstroDatabank is the software that Lois Rodden developed. It contains over thirty thousand birth records, "carefully documented and coded for accuracy with the popular Rodden Rating system. AstroDatabank includes intriguing biographies, revealing personality traits, important life events, and significant relationships." For the curious, the researcher, the neophyte and pro alike.

Both Winstar and SolarFire produce computerized report software. These reports are handy for when a friend of a friend is in a fix and you don't have the time to interpret transits and progressions for the person's birth chart. Winstar also produces software on other divination systems.

Day Watch, another Winstar program, is forecasting software that is invaluable for astrologers. From their site: "Certainly it creates personalized astrological calendars, a great tool for professional astrologers and those who have an understanding of astrological terms, symbols, and technique. But Day Watch also contains a full range of onscreen and printable interpretations of events that even someone with absolutely no astrological training can read, understand, and immediately put to use in their daily lives."

At the beginning of every month we bring up our personalized calendars that tell us what is happening daily in our natal charts and also lists which planets are changing signs in that month, on what date, and which planets are turning retrograde or direct. Each month includes an ephemeris and lunar charts for the new and full moon. The program also offers various types of reports.

Keep in mind that these programs are only for Windows. They don't work with the Mac operating system. As far as we know, there's just one program for Macs—the IO Edition, developed by Time Cycles Research. It lacks the bells and whistles of Winstar, but is certainly good enough for a natal chart and transits.

Getting a Reading

So now you're ready for an astrological reading. But where do you start? Which astrologer should you use?

The best way to find an astrologer is through someone who has gotten a reading and recommends the individual. If you don't know anyone who has had an astrological reading, the next best course is to head over to the nearest bookstore and look through the astrology books. Browse through titles that interest you. Note the author's style. If the author uses a lot of astro jargon or seems to write in a depressing or heavy-handed way, move on. Once you find an author whose book you like, check to see if he or she has a Web site. Most astrologers these days have Web sites that spell out their fees, what types of readings are offered, and a contact address.

Rates for a reading vary from one astrologer to another and usually depend on what you want. Would you like just an interpretation of your natal chart? Would you like a forecast for the next six months or a year? Do you want a compatibility chart for you and your partner? Some astrologers prefer to do phone readings and record the reading. Others prefer to work through e-mail. If the astrologer you've chosen lives close to you, all the better. Have the reading done in person.

What to Expect During a Reading

Every astrological reading begins with your natal chart, so an accurate birth time is essential. It should come from your birth certificate or a parent's memory. An approximate time means the entire reading won't be as accurate. Over the years we've done way too many readings that turned out to be based on inaccurate birth times and then had to construct an accurate chart. If you don't know your time of birth, it's possible to rectify your chart based on major events in your life — the date of your marriage or divorce, a major move, the death of a parent. But this process is time consuming and rarely as accurate as an exact birth time.

A reading with an astrologer differs from a daily horoscope you find in a newspaper or even on a Web site. It's tailored to your specific chart rather than just to your sun sign. If you're getting a reading only on your birth chart, the astrologer interprets the entire chart, not just pieces of it. The astrologer looks at the signs and house placements of the various planets and the angles the planets make to each other.

If you want predictions for the next six or twelve months, the astrologer uses various techniques that are all based on your natal chart. Transits—the daily motion of the planets—have the most immediate impact on our lives, so the astrologer will first look at how the slower-moving planets—Pluto, Neptune, Uranus—impact your chart. Since they stay in the same sign for the greatest length of time, their influence can be felt for decades. The transits of both Saturn and Jupiter are taken into account too.

Usually the astrologer will pay close attention to how the transits of your chart's ruler are affecting you. If you have Scorpio rising, the transits of Pluto and Mars (the coruler) would be important. If you have Gemini rising, Mercury's transits would be important. The astrologer should also consider how eclipses and the new and full moons might affect you, particularly when there's a lunation in the same sign as your natal sun, moon, or rising.

Another predictive technique the astrologer should use is one called progression. In this technique your natal chart is progressed forward in time to the present. Since the moon is the swiftest-moving planet, moving about one progressed degree a month, the progressed chart provides timing. An astrologer can time events down to a month.

Yet another predictive technique is called the solar return chart, where your sun sign is returned to where it was at your birth. This chart's influence extends from one birthday to the next and when compared with the natal chart provides additional information and insights about what you can expect during the next twelve months.

An astrologer may also take a look at other elements in your chart, or if you have a specific question can erect an horary chart for that particular question. Horary and medical astrology are specialized fields and not all astrologers are competent to answer questions using this technique.

CHAPTER 13

By the Numbers

Even though this is an astrology book, we use numbers in some of the daily predictions because we're attempting to remain true to what Sydney Omarr did. The legendary astrologer was also a numerologist and combined the two forms in his work. So let's take a closer look at how the numbers work.

If you're familiar with numerology, you probably know your life path number, which is derived from your birth date. That number represents who you were at birth and the traits that you'll carry throughout your life. There are numerous books and Web sites that provide details on what the numbers mean regarding your life path.

But in the daily predictions, what does it mean when it's a number 9 day, and how did it get to be that number? In the dailies you'll usually find these numbers on the days when the moon is transiting from one sign to another. The system is simple: add the numbers related to the astrological sign (1 for Aries, 2 for Taurus, etc.), the year, the month, and the day.

For example, to find what number June 14, 2014, is

for a Libra, you would start with 7, the number for Libra, add 7 (the number you get when you add 2014 together), plus 6 for June, plus 5 (1+4) for the day. That would be 7+7+6+5 (sign + year + month+ day) = 25 or 7. So June 14, 2014, is a number 7 day for a Libra. It would be an 8 day for a Scorpio, the sign following Libra. So on that number 7 day Libra might be advised that his investigative and research skills are especially strong, and he should explore his spiritual beliefs and venture into the unknown.

Briefly here are the meanings of the numbers, which are included in more detail in the dailies themselves.

1) Taking the lead, getting a fresh start, a new beginning
2) Cooperation, partnership, a new relationship, sensitivity
3) Harmony, beauty, pleasures of life, warm, receptive
4) Getting organized, hard work, being methodical, rebuilding, fulfilling your obligations
5) Freedom of thought and action, change, variety, thinking outside the box
6) A service day, being diplomatic, generous, tolerant, sympathetic
7) Mystery, secrets, investigations, research, detecting deception, exploration of the unknown, of the spiritual realms
8) Your power day, financial success, unexpected money, a windfall
9) Finishing a project, looking beyond the immediate, setting your goals, reflection, expansion.

Simple, right?

Once you become accustomed to what the numbers mean for a particular day, you can adjust your attitude and thoughts accordingly. After all, how a day, week, month, or year unfolds depends more on your attitude toward yourself and your world than it does on any number or astrology sign. If you practice waking up each morning in a spirit of adventure and gratitude, pretty soon it becomes second nature, and your life shifts accordingly. Sound like magical thinking? It is. Try it, and watch your life change.

CHAPTER 14

Matters of the Heart for Capricorn in 2014

As a cardinal earth sign, you tend to be focused, ambitious, directed. When you meet an obstacle, you don't barrel through it, as an Aries might. You simply find your way around it and take an alternate route to get to where you want to go. It's true in every area of your life, even in romance and love. In this chapter we're going to address your emotions, the underpinnings of your personality, particularly where love and romance are concerned.

Whether you're in a relationship or not, astrology is a magnificent tool for alerting you—and the rest of us—when periods are coming up that are favorable or unfavorable for romance. If you're alerted to when challenges may surface, you're better equipped to meet them. The same goes for smooth periods.

In this area we look at the transits of Venus as well as the angles Venus is making to your sun sign. If you know when Venus is making a difficult angle to your sun sign, you can expect challenges in your love life. If you know when Venus is going to be in your sun sign or forming a beneficial angle to it, you can expect a harmonious period.

There are other factors too of course that have a bearing on your love life. What is Mars doing at any given time? As the planet that symbolizes your sexuality, aggression, and ambition, its transits and the angles it makes to Venus and your sun sign are important. Then there are lunar transits. The moon—symbolic of your emotions, inner life, ability to nurture, and intuition— is also important. You can see how this could get complicated very quickly. So for now, let's keep things simple and take a look at the Venus transits in 2014. We'll pinpoint time periods for you that are both terrific and challenging for love, romance, and your creative endeavors.

Venus Transits in 2014 That Make Your Heart Sing

There are three stellar periods this year that are worth noting. Two such periods are when Venus transits your sun sign. Most of us get just one of those periods in 2014, but because of a retrograde between January 1 and 31, you get two of them. The dates when Venus is moving direct in your sign: January 31–March 5 and December 10, 2014, to January 4, 2015.

While Venus transits your sign, you exude great energy and sex appeal, and people clamor for your attention. Your social life picks up considerably. You're very in synch with who you are, and your self-confidence rises. These feelings, in turn, attract new relationship opportunities. Your creative drive is powerful during this period.

The second period to anticipate falls between May

28 and June 23. This time is one of the most romantic and creative for you all year. You're on a roll creatively. Ideas are abundant, and the only thing you have to do is remember to jot them down for future use. Your muse shadows you constantly. If you get involved in a relationship during this period, it's strictly for pleasure. Although it may develop into something later on, you're not focused on commitment just yet. If you're already in a committed relationship, this transit enhances the qualities that brought you two together. You fall in love with each other all over again.

Synchronicity is likely to occur often during these periods, particularly if your life is in transition. Heed whatever messages the synchros bring you.

During all of these transits your earth-sign qualities are enhanced and strengthened. If you're a Capricorn who loves physical activity, you'll be doing more of that—gym workouts, yoga, hiking. If you're focused on the business aspect of your life, you'll be even more so during these transits.

Good Backups

September 5–29: Venus moves through fellow earth sign Virgo, your solar ninth house. This transit favors romance while traveling, in an educational setting, or even while pursuing spiritual studies. Virgo's lively intellect and communications skills suggest that you and your partner won't have any trouble opening up to each other.

April 5–May 2: Venus transits compatible water

sign Pisces, your solar third house. You could meet a romantic interest through a sibling, friends, or a neighbor.

In a romantic relationship, you and your partner may be brainstorming employment possibilities. You would like to be self-employed, but aren't yet sure what the nature of your business might be. You'll figure it out. You always do.

October 23–November 16: Venus transits compatible water sign Scorpio, your solar eleventh house. This one could bring someone interesting into your life through social networks or any groups to which you belong. Even social media sites are possible venues for meeting someone.

July 18–August 12: Venus transits Cancer, your opposite sign. Opposites attract.

Challenging Transits

June 23–July 18: Venus transits air sign Gemini, your solar sixth house. Air and earth aren't compatible, yet Venus in Gemini can enhance your communication abilities and encourage you to be forthright about what you want and expect in a relationship.

September 29–October 23: Venus transits air sign Libra, your solar tenth house. Another air/earth combination. This transit could bring about a romance at work and could be challenging for that reason. Also, Libra is sociable and flirtatious, so the propensity for a work-related romance is possible.

November 16–December 10: Venus transits fire sign Sagittarius, your solar twelfth house. This transit could be challenging in that hidden stuff in a relationship may surface.

When Love Is Serious!

You certainly enjoy your romantic flings, but there are times when you're looking for something more serious and committed. The most favorable time for love as serious business could occur between July 18 and August 12, when Venus transits Cancer, your opposite sign. If you're in a relationship when this transit begins, it could become more serious and committed before the transit ends.

You may find that Jupiter's transit through Cancer, between January 1 and July 16, also favors a deeper commitment and seriousness in a relationship. Jupiter increases whatever it touches, so as it moves through your partnership area, your partnerships expand.

Mark these dates, too: **October 26 to December 4**. Mars transits your sign during this period, so your sexuality is heightened, your physical energy is extraordinary, and there isn't much you *can't* accomplish.

In the next chapter we'll take a look at what Mars is doing this year and how its transits could impact your sexuality.

CHAPTER 15

Your Sexuality and Ambition in 2014

In astrology the planet Mars rules sexuality, physical energy, and your driving ambition to reach particular goals. This planet can also have an indirect impact on your health. So let's take a look at the transits that Mars makes in 2014 and find out which ones may be challenging or beneficial for you.

A positive angle between Mars and your sun sign often acts as a booster rocket—you have more physical energy, drive, and ambition, and your sexuality is heightened. A challenging angle can be frustrating. You may feel things aren't going your way and realize you have to work harder, sleep less, use your time more efficiently. If you're informed about when positive and challenging transits are approaching and how to deal with them, you're empowered. You're better able to cope with the challenges and take advantage of the windows of opportunity.

For the first two months of the year Mars is moving in direct motion in Libra, your solar career area. This transit is a major bonus, when you can make significant professional strides. You might land a promotion or raise or sell your novel or book. You could travel for business, set up an office overseas, get the part you wanted in a play, TV series, a movie. You get the idea here. Set your sights, then go for it.

Between March 1 and May 19 Mars is retrograde. It essentially enters a dormant state, like a bear in the winter, and you can't expect the usual razzle dazzle it produces.

Your energy may not be up to par, you feel less ambitious, less driven. During the retrograde you may revisit sexuality issues you thought were resolved, or your sex life may not be as vigorous as you hoped. Also, social relationships and your team efforts may not go as planned. Something is *off*.

It's easy to feel frustrated when Mars is moving retrograde, and the best way to deal with it is to go the extra mile in everything you do. On the creative front work extra hours on your projects, but only if you enjoy doing so. It's important with this retrograde—and the entire transit—to stick to what you enjoy, what you feel passionate about.

Between May 19 and July 25 it moves in direct motion through Libra again, and you experience the same kind of activity that you did when it was in direct motion earlier in the year.

From July 25 to September 13 Mars transits Scorpio, your solar eleventh house, the area that rules your wishes and dreams, friendships, social networks. Because it's in Scorpio, the transit could stir up stuff that's hidden in these areas. But it also brings tremendous energy, so you may be spending more time with groups and friends, perhaps involved in some sort of group project. It's possible that you become sexually involved with someone in the group. If so, the relationship may be intense.

If you're involved when the transit begins, your relationship goes through an intensely sexual period.

The period from September 13 to October 26, when Mars moves through Sagittarius, your solar twelfth house, indicates that you may be spending time behind the scenes. Or you may be working out of your home or from a spot overseas, but you primarily work in solitude. Since the transit occurs in Sagittarius, a sign that enjoys travel, it's possible that you travel a great deal during this transit. The travel can also be metaphorical—maybe you're in therapy and traveling through your own psyche!

Between October 26 and December 4 Mars transits your sign. The years in which Mars transits your sun sign are usually memorable in some way. Not only is your physical energy excellent, but your sexuality and ambition are greatly enhanced. In fact the two may be intertwined in some way. Power as the greatest aphrodisiac? Be careful, Capricorn, that you don't do something you may regret later!

This transit favors regular exercise. If you don't have a routine yet, start one. If you already exercise, up the ante and try something new—yoga, pilates, Latin dancing.

Between December 4, 2014, and January 12, 2015, Mars transits air sign Aquarius, your solar second house. This transit suggests a lot of frenetic activity related to finances. You may be working harder to make ends meet, or your hard work pays off with a raise or an unexpected payment of some sort.

During this transit your ambition is heightened by

unusual individuals you may meet. They are likely to have unusual ideas and goals that you admire. Your artistic bent becomes more pronounced, so perhaps this is when you decide to follow your heart and do what you love and have faith that the money will follow.

Regardless of your relationship status, your mind is way outside the box during this transit. Seize the ideas as they come to you. They'll prove to be valuable down the road. Aquarius sets trends.

Other Important Dates

On January 1 there's a new moon in your sign, with Pluto and Mercury closely conjunct. Venus is also in your sign. It's a very nice way to start the new year, and the new opportunities that should surface could involve communication, romance, some sort of creative endeavor. Pluto's placement puts you in the power seat, exactly where you like to be.

We also like the new moon in Virgo, your solar ninth house, on August 25. This one should usher in new opportunities to explore your worldview, spiritual beliefs, and your options with publishing and higher education. You may have a chance to travel abroad too.

Keep a Record

In the space below keep a brief record of how each of these transits impacts your life. Over time you may recognize patterns emerging with certain transits of Mars. With access to the Internet, you can also check on how combined transits impact your life.

Let's say that while Mars is moving through a fellow earth sign, a new love relationship begins or a creative project is offered to you. Note the time and date, and then use the Internet to find out what the other planets were doing when this opportunity came along. You may discover that the moon was in your sign or in another earth or water sign.

The purpose of this record is to grasp the patterns to which you're sensitive. If you don't already have a copy of your natal chart, by all means get one. Web sites that offer free natal charts are listed elsewhere in the book. The more information you have, the better prepared you'll be to take advantage of beneficial transits before they arrive!

_____
_____
_____
_____
_____
_____
_____
_____
_____
_____
_____
_____

CHAPTER 16

Career Timing for Capricorn in 2014

Your solar tenth house represents your career, public persona, bosses, and other authoritarian figures. Transits through this house reveal professional challenges and opportunities that may surface. Your solar tenth house falls in Libra, so transits through that sign are moving through your career area. Also, certain transits through your sun sign are important too in terms of professional matters. Now let's take a closer look at what's emerging in your career in 2014.

One of the best dates this year for professional matters falls on September 24, with a new moon in Libra. This new moon should bring new professional opportunities—a promotion, raise, new career, new contacts, a new network of friends and business associates. Your talents and skills will be on display, and coworkers and bosses will recognize you for the valuable employee you are. You may have a chance to take a course or seminar that enhances your professional skills.

However the possibilities unfold for you, *opportunity* is the operative word. Mars in Sagittarius forms a wide, beneficial angle to this new moon, suggesting a lot of activity and forward thrust.

One of the best dates for you in terms of your career and just about everything else occurs on January 1, with a new moon in your sign. Since the moon happens just once every twelve months and sets the tone of things for the next twelve months, it's wise to prepare for it. About a week before the new moon make a list of professional goals, and post it where you'll see it often. Back these goals and desires with strong emotion. Then on the day of the new moon, release them by tossing out the list. Now move aside, and let the universe manifest these desires.

If you've been looking for employment, this new moon could help you find the right job at the right time. You need to do the preliminary work, however. Send out résumés, network, and check Craig's List and other venues for job openings in your field.

Both of Jupiter's transits this year will help you, but in different ways. Between January 1 and July 16, while Jupiter transits Cancer, you may develop new business partnerships. Or you and your personal partner could go into business together. A business partner can also be an accountant, manager, agent, or banker.

While Jupiter moves through fire sign Leo between July 16, 2014, and August 11, 2015, you'll have a chance to showcase your numerous talents and skills. Other people may be more willing to share their resources with you—money, energy, time, expertise. It's possible that you could be delving more deeply into metaphysics during this period.

Synchronicities are likely to occur more frequently

during both of these Jupiter transits, so take the time to understand what the message is.

Between September 29 and October 23 Venus transits Libra, your career area. This period should be quite pleasing. Others are receptive to you and your ideas. Bosses and coworkers find you appealing. You're able to move forward with your projects and find ample support among coworkers. You're a team player. During this period get out there and pitch your ideas, submit manuscripts, network with coworkers. Your communication skills are highlighted, and your conscious mind is quite precise.

Another good period falls between December 16 and January 4, 2015, when Mercury is moving through your sign. Your communication skills are greatly enhanced. It's a great time to pitch ideas, submit manuscripts, network, brainstorm. Your conscious mind is exceptionally organized and efficient during these transits.

When Mars transits your sign between October 26 and December 4, be sure that you tackle difficult issues and challenging projects. It will be easier for you to resolve these issues and move forward with projects that may have stumped you in the past.

A terrific period for creative work falls between May 28 and June 23, when Venus transits Taurus, your solar fifth house. Your muse is ready for intensive, original work, your imagination is geared up, and you're ready to follow your heart and your particular vision. This period is one of the most creative all year, so don't fritter away the opportunity.

The other transit we should mention involves Saturn. Without this planet our lives would lack structure and discipline, and the universe and everything in it would be complete chaos. Between January 1 and March 2 and July 20 and December 23 Saturn is moving direct through compatible water sign Scorpio, your solar eleventh house. This transit helps you to build a strong network of friendships and acquaintances and structures that help you to achieve your wishes and dreams.

Once Saturn enters Sagittarius on December 23, where it will be for the next two and a half years, buried issues will surface that you'll have to deal with and resolve. Your dreams will be a source of insights, information, and inspiration. You'll be clearing out the beliefs, relationships, and issues that no longer serve your best interests, all in preparation for when Saturn enters your sign.

While Saturn is in Sagittarius and transiting the most hidden part of your chart, it's possible that you will spontaneously recall a past life that is most relevant to the issues you're dealing with in this life. It could come through a dream, while you're meditating, or even when you're traveling in a place that seems familiar to you but you've never been before.

If you don't have a meditation practice yet, be sure to start one before Saturn enters Sagittarius, so that you're familiar with how it works and how you can get the most out of it. The periods from September 27 to October 4 and between November 8 and 27 would be a good time to start meditation—or therapy. Mercury is moving direct then, in Scorpio, traveling with Saturn.

Another excellent period for intense inner work falls between October 23 and November 16, when Venus in Scorpio travels with Saturn. It's best to start something new after Mercury turns direct on October 25.

CHAPTER 17

The Big Picture for Capricorn in 2014

Welcome to 2014, Capricorn! It's a 8 year for you. This suggests a year of prosperity and financial gain, a power year.

Now that the tumult of 2012 and the realignment of 2013 are behind you, you're ready to embark on yet another journey. So let's look at how specific areas of your life may be impacted and which dates will be of vital importance to you. We've covered some of this in the previous chapters, but now we'll sum it up for easy reference.

Romance/Creativity

Aren't you lucky! Due to a retrograde of Venus early in the year, 2014 brings you two periods when Venus transits your sign: January 31 to March 5 and December 10, 2014, to January 4, 2015. Venus is retrograde in your sign between January 1 and 31. Let's take a closer look at what all this means.

The Venus retrograde at the beginning of the year

is a continuation from what was going on in December 2013. It suggests some bumps in a romantic relationship, perhaps confusion about finances, and snafus with creative projects. But Venus retros can also bring about physical discomforts in the environment—the heat in your office or home stop working, for instance. Or your new shoes don't fit right. Whatever you do during this period, don't purchase art or jewelry.

During this period your muse is at your beck and call 24/7, and your creative drive is powerful, a magnet that draws the people you need when you need them. New ideas come easily, so be sure to have a recorder or pen and paper handy regardless of where you are. You feel more self-confident during this transit; others pick up on it and are attracted to you, your ideas, persona, and creative projects. So if you have creative products ready, start submitting and exhibiting them, doing whatever you need to do in order to advertise them.

You're in a romantic mood during this transit, and that's true whether you're involved or not. If you're already in a relationship, things between you and your partner should be quite pleasurable, fun, and loving. If you're not involved when the transit begins, you probably will be before the transit ends.

If a relationship begins during this period, it may begin at work or in a work-related setting. This stranger catches your eye; something clicks before you even speak to each other. Perhaps you and this individual work in the same profession or have careers that are allied in some way. You will have similar interests and a solid base for communication. If you're already involved in a relationship, this transit helps to define it.

You and your partner may deepen your commitment to each other.

The other terrific period for romance and creativity occurs between May 28 and June 23, when Venus transits fellow earth sign Taurus, your solar fifth house. This transit urges you to enjoy yourself. What a concept, right? Taurus is a sensual, grounded sign, which moves at its own pace, so the relationship may unfold slowly.

Romantically you're interested in having fun and probably aren't in the frame of mind for anything serious. If you're involved already, you and your partner enjoy a period of near bliss!

Creatively you're at the top of your game and anything you tackle works effortlessly.

Other excellent dates:

April 29 features a solar eclipse in Taurus, your solar fifth house. Mercury is closely conjunct the eclipse degree, suggesting new opportunities to flex your creativity in some form of communication—writing, public speaking. New opportunities surface in romance too. If you're not involved, be sure to get out and socialize and network. That's how you'll meet this new romantic interest.

September 5–29, when Venus transits earth sign Virgo and forms a beneficial angle to your sun. This transit enhances your spirituality and hunger for travel. The travel may involve a spiritual or creative quest of some kind.

Be sure to consult the chapter Matters of the Heart for more details on good dates for romance and creative ventures.

Career

Jupiter's transits through both Cancer and Leo will help every facet of your life, even your career. The caveat with career matters, though, is that if you're doing something you love, you benefit tremendously. If you're working in a field that doesn't excite you, that has become rather humdrum and routine, Jupiter, Mars, Venus, Mercury and your ruler, the moon, could help you to break away and find something that is more aligned with your passions. Be sure to check at one of the online sites suggested earlier in the book to find out when the moon is in your sign each month.

Between January 1 and July 16, Jupiter transits Cancer and your solar seventh house. This transit favors an expansion of your partnerships, both business and personal. In your professional life, this transit could bring the right partner at the right time for a business venture. In love and romance, you and your partner may decide to move in together, get engaged or married.

Between July 16, 2014, and August 11, 2015, Jupiter transits fire sign Leo, your solar eighth house. This could increase your partner's income or result in breaks for you in taxes, insurance, mortgages, or other loans. It could also indicate an inheritance.

Let's take a closer look at the beneficial career times:

September 2–27: Mercury is moving direct in Libra, your career area. This period favors communication with bosses and peers. Pitch your ideas; move all professional matters forward. Start a blog, put up a Web site, advertise your products/services or those of your company. Your communication skills are powerful now.

September 29–October 23: During this period, while Venus transits your career area, you're working steadily and resolutely on a project. Coworkers and bosses are impressed with your ideas and the way you implement them. Others find you so appealing that you're the first to be tapped for team projects. Venus in Libra prompts you to network, socialize, make contacts.

September 24: The new moon in Libra should usher in new professional opportunities. You land a new job, get the interview you've hoped for, are promoted, move into a larger office, sell your book or novel.

Between October 26 and December 4 Mars transits your sign, bringing abundant physical energy and drive. It's the perfect time to tackle challenges.

Finances

Let's look at Venus transits first for beneficial dates for finances. Your solar second house, which rules money, is in Aquarius and there are two periods this year to look for. The first, when Venus is moving direct through Aquarius, occurs between March 5 and April 5. The second period occurs between August 12 and September 5, when Venus transits Leo and your eighth house of shared resources.

During these two transits you may earn extra income, get a raise, take a second job. Your income rises, but your expenses may too. Keep track of your finances.

During the second transit your partner's income may increase, which benefits you as well, and you could get breaks with loans, mortgages, taxes, insurance.

Another beneficial date falls on January 30, with a new moon in Aquarius, your financial area. Uranus forms a close, beneficial angle to this new moon, suggesting a suddenness to events. Maybe a financial windfall? It's a good day to buy a lottery ticket!

Mercury Retrogrades

Every year Mercury—the planet of communication and travel—turns retrograde three times. During these periods it's wise not to sign contracts (unless you don't mind renegotiating when Mercury is moving direct), to check and recheck travel plans, and to communicate as succinctly as possible. Refrain from buying any large-ticket items or electronics during this time too. Often computers and appliances go on the fritz, cars act up, data is lost . . . you get the idea. Be sure to back up all files before the dates below:

February 6–28: Mercury retrograde in Pisces, your solar third house of travel and communication. It slips back into Aquarius before it turns direct, so your financial area is also impacted.

June 7–July 1: Mercury retrograde in Cancer, your solar eighth house. This retrograde affects shared resources—your partner's income, mortgages, loans, insurance. In other words, don't apply for loans during this retrograde. Since the retro is in Cancer, it may also impact the people who nurture you and those whom you nurture.

October 4–25: Mercury retrograde in Scorpio. This one impacts your solar eleventh house, so don't be surprised if old issues—and relationships—surface.

Eclipses

Solar eclipses tend to trigger external events that bring about change according to the sign and house in which they fall. Lunar eclipses trigger inner, emotional events according to the sign and house in which they fall. Any eclipse marks both beginnings and endings. The solar and lunar eclipse in a pair falls in opposite signs. If you're interested in detailed information on eclipses, take a look at Celeste Teal's excellent and definitive book, *Eclipses: Predicting World Events & Personal Transformation.*

If you were born under or around the time of an eclipse, it's to your advantage to take a look at your birth chart to find out exactly where the eclipses will impact you.

Most years feature four eclipses—two solar, two lunar—with the set separated by about two weeks. Let's take a closer look.

April 15: Lunar eclipse in Libra, your solar tenth house. Your career or professional life stirs up emotions.

April 29: Solar eclipse in Taurus, your solar fifth house. New opportunities surface in your creativity and romance.

October 8: Lunar eclipse in Aries, your solar fourth house. Uranus is closely conjunct the moon, so you can expect sudden and unexpected emotional issues related to your domestic environment.

October 23: Solar eclipse in Scorpio, your solar eleventh house. New opportunities surface with friends and your wishes and dreams.

The Luckiest Days of 2014

Every year there are one or two days when Jupiter and the sun meet up, and luck, serendipity, and expansion are the hallmarks. This year those days fall on July 25–26. Circle the dates. Do whatever you enjoy!

CHAPTER 18

Eighteen Months of Day-by-Day Predictions: July 2013 to December 2014

Moon sign times are calculated for Eastern Standard Time and Eastern Daylight Time. Please adjust for your local time zone.

JULY 2013

Monday, July 1 (Moon into Taurus, 4:44 p.m.)   It's a number 6 day. Service to others is the theme of the day. You offer advice and support. Focus on making people happy, but don't spread yourself too thin. Be understanding, and avoid confrontations.

Tuesday, July 2 (Moon in Taurus)   The moon is in your fifth house today. Your emotions tend to overpower your intellect. Be yourself; be emotionally honest. In love there's greater emotional depth to a relationship now. You feel strongly attached to loved ones, particularly children. But eventually you need to let go.

Wednesday, July 3 (Moon in Taurus)   Under the influence of the Taurus moon, you tend to focus on practical matters. Cultivate new ideas, but make sure that they're down to earth. Be aware that you might be somewhat stubborn and resistant to change. While you maintain a common-sense, down-to-earth perspective on life today, you also long for the good life with its material blessings.

Thursday, July 4 (Moon into Gemini, 4:23 a.m.) It's a number 9 day. Clear up odds and ends. Make room for something new, but don't start a project until tomorrow. Look beyond the immediate. Visualize the future. Set your goals, then make them so.

Friday, July 5 (Moon in Gemini)   The moon is in your sixth house today. It's a service day. You could be feeling sensitive now and emotionally down. Help others where you can, but avoid falling into a martyr syndrome. Take care of any health issues, and get ready for a big day tomorrow.

Saturday, July 6 (Moon into Cancer, 5:14 p.m.) Your intuition focuses on relationships today. Trust your feelings, but don't make waves. Don't rush or show resentment; let things develop. The spotlight is on cooperation. Emotions and sensitivity are highlighted. Show your appreciation to others.

Sunday, July 7 (Moon in Cancer)   Saturn turns direct in your eleventh house, where it stays until December 24 of next year. That means that over the coming months issues could develop related to your involvement in a group. You also could face difficulties in dealing with matters related to friends and associates. Keep close tabs on your emotions, especially when in front of the public. You feel most comfortable working at home out of public view.

Monday, July 8 (Moon in Cancer) There's a new moon and four planets in your seventh house now. That could mean you get an opportunity for a contract. It could relate to a partner, who plays a role. Women play a prominent role.

Tuesday, July 9 (Moon into Leo, 5:48 a.m.) It's a number 5 day. Promote new ideas; get ready for change. You can overcome obstacles with ease. Variety is the spice of life. Freedom of action and thought is emphasized. Let go of old structures.

Wednesday, July 10 (Moon in Leo) The moon is in your eighth house today. You gain financially through a marriage or partnership. You express strong convictions, but you feel best working behind the scenes. Try your best to avoid any jealousies that arise.

Thursday, July 11 (Moon into Virgo, 5:12 p.m.) Get ready for a journey into the unknown. Secrets, intrigue, confidential information play a role. Knowledge is essential to success. Gather information, but avoid making any absolute decisions for the time being. You work best on your own today.

Friday, July 12 (Moon in Virgo) The moon is in your ninth house today. You're a dreamer and a thinker. You may feel a need to get away now, a break from the routine. Higher education or long-distance travel could play a role. You might sign up now for a workshop or seminar.

Saturday, July 13 (Moon in Virgo)   Mars moves into your seventh house today. You take action related to a partnership. You can be quite forceful or aggressive. It's best to go out of your way to be cooperative. You gain from a partnership, especially one that is based in your home.

Sunday, July 14 (Moon into Libra, 2:41 a.m.)   It's a number 1 day. You're at the top of your cycle. You get a fresh start. Your intuition is highlighted. You're inventive and make connections that others overlook. Get out and meet new people. You attract creative individuals now. Explore and discover.

Monday, July 15 (Moon in Libra)   The moon is in your tenth house today. You gain an elevation in prestige. Your hard work pays off. Your life is more public, so make sure you keep your emotions under control while in the public eye. You get along well with coworkers, but it's best now to keep your professional and personal lives separate.

Tuesday, July 16 (Moon into Scorpio, 9:25 a.m.) It's a number 3 day. Stay optimistic. Remain flexible today. Your vitality and natural ability to express yourself are emphasized. Follow your intuition. Expect an invitation from a friend or loved one.

Wednesday, July 17 (Moon in Scorpio)   Uranus goes retrograde in your fourth house today, where it stays until December 17. That means you might be doing some soul searching related to matters in your home. You could be getting flashes of inspiration related to a home-repair project. You could also be dealing with a parent or parents more over the next few months.

Thursday, July 18 (Moon into Sagittarius, 12:55 p.m.)
Promote new ideas; get ready for change. You can overcome obstacles with ease. Variety is the spice of life. Freedom of action and thought is emphasized. Let go of old structures; get a new point of view.

Friday, July 19 (Moon in Sagittarius)   The moon is in your twelfth house today. It's a good time to step back and withdraw from the action. Keep your feelings secret as you work behind the scenes. Relations with women can be difficult now. It's a great day for a mystical or spiritual discipline. Your intuition is heightened.

Saturday, July 20 (Moon into Capricorn, 1:40 p.m.)
Mercury goes direct in your seventh house. That means that any confusion, miscommunication, and delays that you've been experiencing related to a partnership, either personal or business, recede into the past. Things move more smoothly now related to a contract. You get your message across, and everything works better, including computers and other electronic equipment. You get along well with coworkers. At the same time you keep your emotions to yourself.

Sunday, July 21 (Moon in Capricorn)   With the moon in your first house and on your ascendant, you get your batteries recharged. You're physically vital, Capricorn, and get along well with the opposite sex. You're also malleable and easily change your mind. You're restless and uncertain what to do.

Monday, July 22 (Moon into Aquarius, 1:08 p.m.)
Venus moves into your ninth house today, where it stays until August 16. It's a good time for planning or taking a long-distance journey or pursuing higher education. You might take a seminar or workshop in a subject of interest. A foreign-born person could play a role. Meanwhile, there's a full moon in your second house. That means you reap what you've sown, especially related to finances. It's time to harvest the fruits of your efforts.

Tuesday, July 23 (Moon in Aquarius)   The moon is in your second house. Money and material goods are important to you now and give you a sense of security, Capricorn. You may be dealing with payments and collecting what's owed to you. Look at your priorities in handling your income. Expect emotional experiences related to money.

Wednesday, July 24 (Moon into Pisces, 1:23 p.m.)
It's a number 2 day. Use your intuition to get a sense of your day. Be kind and understanding. Cooperation, especially with partners, is highlighted. Don't make waves. Don't rush or show resentment; let things develop. Marriage plays a key role.

Thursday, July 25 (Moon in Pisces)   The moon is in your third house today. Take what you know, and share it with others. Look forward to a visit from relatives or siblings, but keep conscious control of your emotions. Your thinking is unduly influenced by things of the past.

Friday, July 26 (Moon into Aries, 4:30 p.m.)   Stick to practical matters today. You're seen as trustworthy and down to earth by others now. Stay with this energy, Capricorn, and avoid any overly aggressive behavior. You can gain recognition, success, and fame for your hard work.

Saturday, July 27 (Moon in Aries)   The moon is in your fourth house today. Get organized, Capricorn. You're dealing with foundations, the very foundations of who you are and who you are becoming. Make an effort to change a bad habit. It's best to work on your own. Stay focused, and don't get distracted.

Sunday, July 28 (Moon into Taurus, 11:44 p.m.) It's a number 6 day. A domestic adjustment works out for the best. You could face emotional outbursts or someone making unfair demands. Be understanding, and avoid confrontations. Offer advice and support, but do it in a diplomatic way.

Monday, July 29 (Moon in Taurus)   With the moon in your fifth house today, it's a good day to take a chance, experiment. Be aware that your emotions tend to overpower your intellect now. You're emotionally in touch with your creative side. Alternately, you are more protective and nurturing toward children.

Tuesday, July 30 (Moon in Taurus)   Under the
influence of the Taurus moon, you can cultivate new
ideas. But make sure that they are down to earth. Be
aware that you might be somewhat stubborn and resistant to change. Health and physical activity are
highlighted. It's also a good time for gardening, cultivating ideas, doing practical things.

Wednesday, July 31 (Moon into Gemini, 10:42 a.m.)
It's a number 9 day. Look beyond the immediate,
Capricorn. Finish what you started. Visualize the future; set your goals, then make them so. Complete a
project, and make room for something new.

AUGUST 2013

Thursday, August 1 (Moon in Gemini)   With the
moon in your sixth house today, the emphasis turns to
your daily work and helping others. Attend to details,
and be careful not to overlook any seemingly minor
matters that could take on importance. Keep up with
your exercise plan, and watch your diet.

Friday, August 2 (Moon into Cancer, 11:30 p.m.)
It's a number 8 day, and that means it's your power
day; you're in the power seat. You attract financial
success. You have a chance to expand, to gain recognition, fame, power. You're playing with power, so be
careful not to hurt others.

Saturday, August 3 (Moon in Cancer)   The moon
is in your seventh house today. The focus turns to relationships, business and personal ones. You get along

well with others. You can fit in just about anywhere. Loved ones and partners are more important than usual. A legal matter comes to your attention now. It could be a marriage.

Sunday, August 4 (Moon in Cancer) Under the influence of the Cancer moon, you could feel moody today and overly sensitive. It might seem as if the world is out to get you. It's not. Get out and take a walk. Beautify your home. Snuggle with a loved one.

Monday, August 5 (Moon into Leo, 11:58 a.m.) It's a number 2 day. It's all about partnerships, cooperation, working together to get things done. Look for a new relationship to develop. Use your intuition to get a sense of how it will work out. Help comes through friends.

Tuesday, August 6 (Moon in Leo) There's a new moon in your eighth house today. That could mean new opportunities come your way related to a partner's assets. Shared income or finances play an important role. With Uranus trine to the moon, you gain sudden insight, and your dreams are vivid.

Wednesday, August 7 (Moon into Virgo, 10:58 p.m.) It's a number 4 day. That means you're building foundations for an outlet for your creativity. Emphasize quality related to whatever you're working on. Persevere to get things done today, Capricorn. Tear down the old in order to rebuild, but do so carefully. Avoid reckless behavior.

Thursday, August 8 (Moon in Virgo)   With Mercury moving into your eighth house today, there's lots of communication between you and a partner or spouse about shared possessions or finances over the next three weeks. You're dealing with a mortgage, insurance, credit cards, possibly an inheritance or taxes.

Friday, August 9 (Moon in Virgo)   The moon is in your ninth house. You're a dreamer and a thinker. You may feel a need to get away now, a break from the usual routine. Foreigners or a foreign country could be involved in your day. You also take a renewed interest in religion, mythology, or philosophy. The law or publishing could play a role.

Saturday, August 10 (Moon into Libra, 8:09 a.m.) It's a number 7 day. You work best on your own today. Gather information, but don't make any absolute decisions until tomorrow. Go with the flow. Avoid confusion and conflicts. Keep any secrets entrusted to you.

Sunday, August 11 (Moon in Libra)   The moon is in your tenth house today. Professional concerns take on more importance. You could get a promotion, raise, or pat on the back. You're more responsive to the needs and moods of a group and of the public in general. You move up the ladder.

Monday, August 12 (Moon into Scorpio, 3:19 p.m.) Clear your desk for tomorrow's new cycle. Accept what comes your way now. Use the day for reflection, expansion, and concluding projects. Don't start anything new today.

Tuesday, August 13 (Moon in Scorpio) The moon is in your eleventh house today, Capricorn. Your friendships expand now as new people come into your life. You find strength in numbers and meaning through friends and groups. Focus on your wishes and dreams. Take a close look at your responsibilities and obligations, and follow through on them. Make sure that you're not hurting anyone with whatever you're doing.

Wednesday, August 14 (Moon into Sagittarius, 8:05 p.m.) Your intuition focuses on relationships, either a new one that's developing or a current one. Don't make waves. Don't rush or show resentment; let things develop. Cooperation is highlighted. You work well with others. Show your appreciation to others.

Thursday, August 15 (Moon in Sagittarius) The moon is in your twelfth house today. It's a good day to withdraw and work behind the scenes. Think carefully before you act. There's a tendency now to undo all the positive actions you've taken. Avoid any self-destructive behavior. Be aware of hidden enemies.

Friday, August 16 (Moon into Capricorn, 10:26 p.m.) Venus moves into your ninth house today. You feel good about your studies now, especially your interest in philosophy, religion, art, or art history. It's a great time for long-distance travel for pleasure and romance. You're especially intuitive and enjoy the finer things in life.

Saturday, August 17 (Moon in Capricorn) The moon is on your ascendant today. Your face is in front of the public. You're recharged for the remainder of the month, and that makes you more appealing to the public. You're physically vital, and relations with the opposite sex go well. The way you see yourself now is the way others see you.

Sunday, August 18 (Moon into Aquarius, 11:07 p.m.) It's a number 6 day. That means service to others is the theme of the day. Offer your advice and support. Diplomacy wins the way. Be sympathetic and kind, generous and tolerant. Do a good deed for someone.

Monday, August 19 (Moon in Aquarius) The moon is in your second house today. Money issues and your emotions are on your agenda. Money and material goods are important to you now and give you a sense of security. You identify emotionally with your possessions or whatever you value. You feel best when surrounded by familiar objects. It's not the objects that are important, but the feelings and memories you associate with them. Put off making any major purchases.

Tuesday, August 20 (Moon into Pisces, 11:44 p.m.) Things turn around today with the full moon in your second house. Now you find your answers—illumination, insight—just what you were looking for. Security, money, and material goods are important to you. Collect what's owed you. Pay what you owe, and put off making any major purchases now.

Wednesday, August 21 (Moon in Pisces) The moon is in your third house today. Your mental abilities are strong, and you have an emotional need to express your ideas. Your thinking is unduly influenced by things of the past. A short trip works to your benefit.

Thursday, August 22 (Moon in Pisces)   Under the influence of the Pisces moon, you can tap deeply into the collective unconscious for inspiration. Imagination is highlighted. Watch for psychic events, synchronicities. Keep track of your dreams, including your daydreams. Ideas are ripe.

Friday, August 23 (Moon into Aries, 2:13 a.m.) It's all about partnerships, cooperation, working together to get things done today. Look for a new relationship to develop. Use your intuition to get a sense of how it will work out. Help comes through friends.

Saturday, August 24 (Moon in Aries)   The moon is in your fourth house today. Spend time with your family and other loved ones; stick close to home. Work on a home-repair project. Beautify your surroundings. You feel a close tie to your roots. A parent could play an important role in your day.

Sunday, August 25 (Moon into Taurus, 8:14 a.m.) It's a number 4 day. That means the emphasis is on your organizational skills. In romance your persistence pays off. You're building a foundation for the future. Be methodical and thorough. Fulfill your obligations. Emphasize quality.

Monday, August 26 (Moon in Taurus)   With the moon in your fifth house today, sex for pleasure is highlighted, Capricorn. It's also a good day to take a chance, experiment. You move ahead on a creative project. Children and pets play a role in your day.

Tuesday, August 27 (Moon into Gemini, 6:08 p.m.) Mars moves into your eighth house today and stays there until October 15. Your ability to investigate important matters is strong over the coming weeks. You're also very persuasive now, especially when you're promoting your own ideas. However, watch your temper if you encounter resistance. It's also a good time for long-distance travel. You're in an adventurous mood this summer.

Wednesday, August 28 (Moon in Gemini) The moon is in your sixth house today. Delegate some of your responsibilities; avoid taking on too much work. You help others, but allow them to shoulder some of the burden. Don't become a martyr for other people's causes. Take care of any health issues.

Thursday, August 29 (Moon in Gemini) Under the influence of the Gemini moon, your mind is surprisingly facile today, Capricorn. You get your ideas across and are busy sending messages or talking on the phone. You're looking for intellectual stimulation, but you tend to analyze and rationalize too much. It's a good day to socialize with friends. Get out and have fun; flirt with someone new.

Friday, August 30 (Moon into Cancer, 6:33 a.m.) Complete a project now. Clear up loose ends. Visualize the future. Set your goals, then make them so. Take an inventory on where things are going in your life. It's a good day to make a donation to a worthy cause.

Saturday, August 31 (Moon in Cancer) The moon is in your seventh house today. The focus turns to relationships, business and personal ones. You're looking for security and feel a need to be accepted. Be careful that others don't manipulate your feelings. Women play a prominent role now.

SEPTEMBER 2013

Sunday, September 1 (Moon into Leo, 7:02 p.m.) It's a number 8 day, your power day and your day to play it your way. You can go far with your plans and achieve financial success. You have a chance to expand, to gain recognition, fame, power.

Monday, September 2 (Moon in Leo) The moon is in your eighth house today. You attract the attention of powerful people, Capricorn. Be aware that your experiences could be more intense than usual. You could be dealing with a matter related to shared belongings, investments, or taxes. An interest in metaphysics plays a role. You could be reading about concepts of life after death.

Tuesday, September 3 (Moon in Leo) Under the influence of the Leo moon, there's high drama in the air as security becomes an important issue for you. Your sense of duty and obligation can affect your feelings about shared belongings. Matters of sex, death and rebirth, rituals, and relationships emerge now.

Wednesday, September 4 (Moon into Virgo, 5:45 a.m.)   Cooperation is highlighted today. Use your intuition to get a sense of your day. Be kind and understanding. Show your appreciation to others. There could be some soul searching related to relationships.

Thursday, September 5 (Moon in Virgo)   There's a new moon in your ninth house today. That could mean you get an opportunity now for long-distance travel or continuing your education . . . or both. A foreign-born person or a foreign country plays a role. With Jupiter forming a sextile, worldviews are emphasized, and you have an opportunity to expand your plans.

Friday, September 6 (Moon into Libra, 2:14 p.m.) It's a number 4 day, Capricorn, your kind of day. Hard work and persistence are called for in order to get ahead. Make use of your organizational skills. Be methodical and thorough, and stay on task. You're building a base for your future. Be aware that you could feel overworked.

Saturday, September 7 (Moon in Libra)   With the moon in your tenth house, you take your professional life into the weekend. You know you deserve a raise or advancement or both. Your life is more in public view now. Your hard work is appreciated, Capricorn.

Sunday, September 8 (Moon into Scorpio, 8:45 p.m.) It's a number 6 day. Domestic purchases are highlighted. It's a service day, so direct your energy toward helping others, Capricorn. Focus on making people happy. Do a good deed. Be generous and tolerant, even if it goes against your nature.

Monday, September 9 (Moon in Scorpio)   Mercury moves into your tenth house today. Your speaking and writing abilities flourish now. You communicate well to the public, and your efforts bolster your career. You gain recognition for what you do.

Tuesday, September 10 (Moon in Scorpio)   With the moon in your eleventh house today, friends play an important role, especially Taurus and Virgo. Take a look at your goals, and make sure that they're still an expression of who you are. You do well in a group setting. You could be dealing with an issue involving social consciousness.

Wednesday, September 11 (Moon into Sagittarius, 1:36 a.m.)   Venus moves into your eleventh house today. Social activities are highlighted, possibly in your own home. You get along well with others and put new acquaintances at ease. You work smoothly with a group now and show your affection to friends.

Thursday, September 12 (Moon in Sagittarius) The moon is in your twelfth house today. Unconscious attitudes can be difficult; so can relations with women. Keep your feelings to yourself now. Be aware of hidden enemies. It's a great day for a mystical or spiritual discipline. Your intuition is heightened.

Friday, September 13 (Moon into Capricorn, 4:56 a.m.)   Partnerships, both personal and business, are more important than usual. Marriage plays a key role. Help comes through friends, especially loved ones. Show your appreciation to others.

Saturday, September 14 (Moon in Capricorn)
With the moon on your ascendant, you get recharged for the remainder of the month, and this makes you more appealing to the public. You're physically vital, and relations with the opposite sex go well. It's all about your health and emotional self: how you feel and how you feel about yourself. Your feelings tend to fluctuate by the moment.

Sunday, September 15 (Moon into Aquarius, 7:06 a.m.) It's a number 4 day. It's time to get things organized for the week ahead, Capricorn. Revise, rewrite. Clean a closet, garage, or attic. Be methodical and thorough. Be practical with your money.

Monday, September 16 (Moon in Aquarius) With the moon in your second house today, you could gain a financial boost that feels like a jolt of energy. Money and material goods are important to you now and give you a sense of security. However, you need to decide your priorities in handling your income. Temper your spending, take care of payments, and create a plan. Follow your values, or focus on whatever you value.

Tuesday, September 17 (Moon into Pisces, 8:59 a.m.)
It's a number 6 day. Domestic purchases are highlighted. Focus on making people happy. Do a good

deed. It's a service day, so direct your energy toward helping others, Capricorn. Be generous and tolerant, even if it goes against your nature.

Wednesday, September 18 (Moon in Pisces) The moon is in your third house today. Your mental abilities are strong now, and you have an emotional need to reinvigorate your studies, especially regarding matters of the past. You're attracted to historical studies or prehistorical explorations. Take what you know, and share it with others. You could be getting involved in a challenging mental activity, such as on-line gaming, a debate, or a game of chess.

Thursday, September 19 (Moon into Aries, 11:58 a.m.) There's a full moon today in your third house. You gain better understanding about a matter from the past. Your curiosity reaps results. You can expand on any plans involving siblings, other family members, or neighbors. As you go about your everyday life, look to the past for clues about what's coming up in the near future.

Friday, September 20 (Moon in Aries) With Pluto going direct in your first house, Capricorn, you're likely to face profound transformation related to your personal life over the next ten years. It could mean that you become famous, or at least your face becomes well known. The reason behind your public profile could relate to overcoming great odds, or it could result from a notorious act on your part. Either way the change will be dramatic.

Saturday, September 21 (Moon into Taurus, 5:34 p.m.) It's a number 1 day, and you're at the top of your cycle. Stress originality. Explore, discover, create. Express your opinions dynamically, but refuse to deal with people who have closed minds. A flirtation turns more serious.

Sunday, September 22 (Moon in Taurus) The moon is in your fifth house today. Be yourself; be emotionally honest. In love there's greater emotional depth to a relationship now. You're emotionally in touch with your creative side. In fact, your emotions tend to overpower your intellect. You're more protective and nurturing toward children.

Monday, September 23 (Moon in Taurus) Under the influence of the Taurus moon, your health and physical activity are highlighted. Go hiking; get out in nature. It's a good time for doing practical things, cultivating ideas. Try to avoid stubborn behavior when others question your actions. You could be somewhat possessive now. While you maintain a common-sense, down-to-earth perspective on life, you also long for the good life with its material blessings.

Tuesday, September 24 (Moon into Gemini, 2:35 a.m.) It's a number 4 day. Persevere to get things done today. Tear down the old in order to rebuild. You're building a creative base for your future. Be methodical and thorough. Missing papers or objects are found.

Wednesday, September 25 (Moon in Gemini) With the moon in your sixth house today, the emphasis turns to your daily work and service to others. Attend to all the details, Capricorn. Be careful not to overlook any seemingly minor matters that could take on importance. Keep up with your exercise plan, and watch your diet.

Thursday, September 26 (Moon into Cancer, 2:25 p.m.)   Service to others is the theme of the day. You offer advice and support. Do a good deed for someone. Focus on making people happy. Domestic purchases are highlighted.

Friday, September 27 (Moon in Cancer)   The moon is in your seventh house today. The focus turns to relationships, business and personal ones. You get along well with others now. You comprehend the nuances of a situation, but it's difficult to go with the flow. Be careful that others don't manipulate your feelings.

Saturday, September 28 (Moon in Cancer)   Under the influence of the Cancer moon, your family and personal environment take on more importance. It's a good day to plan or work on a home-improvement project. Take plenty of breaks today from your work. That will help you clear your head and improve your focus when you return to work.

Sunday, September 29 (Moon into Leo, 2:58 a.m.) Mercury moves into your eleventh house today. Your mind is quick now, and you pursue a variety of ideas. You communicate well with members of a group. Friends provide you with a variety of opinions and a wide range of perspectives.

Monday, September 30 (Moon in Leo)   The moon is in your eighth house today. You could be attracting powerful people to your cause. Your experiences could be intense, especially related to shared belongings. An interest in metaphysics plays a role.

OCTOBER 2013

Tuesday, October 1 (Moon into Virgo, 1:53 p.m.) The month begins on a number 9 day. Finish what you've started. Visualize the future; set your goals, then make them so. Clear up odds and ends. Take an inventory on where things are going in your life. It's a good day to make a donation to a worthy cause.

Wednesday, October 2 (Moon in Virgo)   The moon is in your ninth house today. You're feeling as if you need to get away. Your mind is active, and you yearn for new experiences, a break from the routine. Plan a trip or sign up for a seminar or workshop. A foreign country or person of foreign birth could play a role.

Thursday, October 3 (Moon into Libra, 10:00 p.m.) Help comes through friends. A partner or lover plays a role. Focus on your direction, your motivation. Where are you going and why? The spotlight is on cooperation. Show your appreciation to others. Partners are highlighted.

Friday, October 4 (Moon in Libra)   There's a new moon in your tenth house today. New opportunities arise now related to your career or profession. You get a raise or promotion, a boost in status. You get along well with fellow workers, and your life is more public.

Saturday, October 5 (Moon in Libra)   Under the influence of the Libra moon, romance is highlighted. This is a great day to schedule an adventurous encounter with your significant other. Your friend is as excited and enthusiastic about the day as you are.

Sunday, October 6 (Moon into Scorpio, 3:33 a.m.) It's a number 5 day. Variety is the spice of life. Think outside the box. Take risks, experiment. Release old structures; get a new point of view. You're versatile, changeable. However, be careful not to spread out and diversify too much.

Monday, October 7 (Moon in Scorpio)   Venus moves into your twelfth house, where it stays until November 5. You love your solitude today, a chance to get away from all the noise and chaos of daily life. You could be secretly admiring someone, especially a person who seems disadvantaged. But you're still unwilling to share your thoughts.

Tuesday, October 8 (Moon into Sagittarius, 7:22 a.m.) There's an air of mystery in your day. Look beneath the surface, investigate. Confidential information plays a role. Knowledge is essential to success. See things as they are and not how you wish them to be. You see the big picture now, not just the details.

Wednesday, October 9 (Moon in Sagittarius)   The moon is in your twelfth house today. It's a good day to withdraw and spend time in private. Relax and meditate. Keep your feelings to yourself, unless you confide in a close friend. Follow your intuition. It's a great day for a mystical or spiritual discipline.

Thursday, October 10 (Moon into Capricorn, 10:18 a.m.)   Visualize your future. Reconsider your goals. Make sure they reflect the person you are becoming, Capricorn. Strive for universal appeal. You're up to the challenge. Complete projects, and make room for the new.

Friday, October 11 (Moon in Capricorn)   The moon is in your first house today. You're feeling somewhat sensitive to other people's feelings. You may feel moody—withdrawn one moment, happy the next, then sad. It's all about your emotional self. Your feelings and thoughts are aligned.

Saturday, October 12 (Moon into Aquarius, 1:00 p.m.)   Use your intuition to get a sense of your day. Be kind and understanding. The spotlight is on cooperation. Marriage plays a key role now. Show your appreciation to others.

Sunday, October 13 (Moon in Aquarius)   Expect emotional experiences related to money and your values. It's a good day for investments, but be practical. Don't make any major purchases now. You seek financial and domestic security, and you feel best surrounded by familiar objects.

Monday, October 14 (Moon into Pisces, 4:06 p.m.)
It's a number 4 day. Put your organizational skills to use today. Revise and rewrite. Tear down in order to rebuild. Be methodical and thorough. Stay focused, and emphasize quality. You're in the right place at the right time.

Tuesday, October 15 (Moon in Pisces) The moon is in your third house today, Capricorn. You're a dreamer and a thinker. You may feel a need to get away now, a break from the usual routine. Pursue a new idea. Are you ready to plan a long trip?

Wednesday, October 16 (Moon into Aries, 8:19 p.m.)
It's a number 6 day. You offer advice and support. Diplomacy wins the way. Be sympathetic and kind, generous and tolerant. A domestic adjustment works out for the best. Be understanding, and avoid confrontations.

Thursday, October 17 (Moon in Aries) The moon is in your fourth house today. Look for some quiet time for meditation. Tend to domestic duties; work on a plan to improve or beautify your house. Spend time with loved ones, especially if you've ignored them recently.

Friday, October 18 (Moon in Aries) There's a lunar eclipse in your fourth house today. You have a strong emotional reaction to something going on in your home. Try to stay in control of your emotions when communicating. Take time to retreat to a private place for meditation. A parent might play a role in your day.

Saturday, October 19 (Moon into Taurus, 2:28 a.m.)
It's a number 9 day. Finish what you've started. Visualize the future; set your goals, then make them so. Clear up odds and ends. Take an inventory on where things are going in your life. It's a good day to make a donation to a worthy cause.

Sunday, October 20 (Moon in Taurus)   The moon is in your fifth house today. You feel a sudden surge of inspiration, a creative urge that helps you break through a block. In romance there's more depth and understanding in a relationship. Children play an important role in your day.

Monday, October 21 (Moon into Gemini, 11:15 a.m.)   Mercury goes retrograde in your eleventh house today and stays there until November 10. Computer glitches over the next three weeks could affect matters related to your involvement in a group activity. You can expect some miscommunication with friends and associates. If you're involved in a group effort aimed at improving the welfare of others, there could be some delays.

Tuesday, October 22 (Moon in Gemini)   The moon is in your sixth house today. It's another service day. Others rely on you for help. So what else is new! Help them, but don't deny your own needs. Visit someone who is ill; do a good deed. Pay attention to any health matters now. Exercise, and watch your diet.

Wednesday, October 23 (Moon into Cancer, 10:37 p.m.)   It's a number 4 day. Put your organizational skills to use today. Revise and rewrite. Tear down in order to rebuild. Be methodical and thorough. Stay focused, and emphasize quality. You're in the right place at the right time.

Thursday, October 24 (Moon in Cancer)   The moon is in your seventh house today. The focus turns to relationships, business and personal ones. You get along well with others now. You can fit in just about anywhere. Loved ones and partners are more important than usual. A legal matter comes to your attention.

Friday, October 25 (Moon in Cancer)   Under the influence of the Cancer moon, you're more sensitive to other people's moods. It's best to keep some things to yourself. Get out and take a walk. Your home environment takes on more importance to you. Make an effort to beautify your home.

Saturday, October 26 (Moon into Leo, 11:13 a.m.) It's your mystery day, Capricorn. You take a journey into the unknown. Look beneath the surface, investigate. Confidential information plays a role. Dig deep for clues. See things as they are and not how you wish them to be.

Sunday, October 27 (Moon in Leo)   The moon is in your eighth house today. Your ambition and drive to succeed are highlighted. Your responsibilities increase; you may feel stressed, overworked.

Monday, October 28 (Moon into Virgo, 10:45 p.m.) It's a number 9 day. Complete what you've been working on, and get ready for something new. Consider ways to expand. Reflect on everything that has happened recently, and follow your intuitive nudges. A new cycle is about to begin.

Tuesday, October 29 (Moon in Virgo)   The moon is in your ninth house today. You're feeling a need to get away. Your mind is active, and you yearn for new experiences, a break from the routine. Plan a trip or sign up for a seminar or workshop. A foreign country or person of foreign birth could play a role.

Wednesday, October 30 (Moon in Virgo)   Under the influence of the Virgo moon, you might be focusing on your health and diet. Stop worrying and fretting. Stick close to home. Attend to the details and loose ends. Take time to write in a journal. You write from a deep place now with lots of details and colorful descriptions.

Thursday, October 31 (Moon into Libra, 7:22 a.m.)
It's a number 3 day. Take time to relax, enjoy yourself, and recharge your batteries for the month ahead. You can influence people now with your upbeat attitude and natural ability to express yourself. Make time to listen to others. Remain flexible.

NOVEMBER 2013

Friday, November 1 (Moon in Libra)   The moon is in your tenth house today. Focus on your professional concerns as the week ends. You could be dealing with bosses and others in power. You can be more responsive to the needs and moods of others around you now. You keep everyone grounded, Capricorn, but make sure you stay grounded yourself. A word of caution: an office romance could be dangerous.

Saturday, November 2 (Moon into Scorpio, 1:35 p.m.)   You could be undergoing some soul searching related to a relationship now. Help comes through friends or loved ones, especially a partner. Don't make waves. Don't rush or show resentment; let things develop. The spotlight is on cooperation.

Sunday, November 3 — Daylight Saving Time Ends (Moon in Scorpio)   There's a solar eclipse in your eleventh house today. That means new opportunities come your way related to friends, associates, or a group. With four planets also in Scorpio, everything is enhanced — for better or worse — especially issues related to your efforts to stress your individuality. It's the beginning or end of something that could relate to your wishes and dreams.

Monday, November 4 (Moon into Sagittarius, 3:14 p.m.)   It's a number 4 day — your kind of day, Capricorn. Your organizational skills are highlighted. Control your impulses. Fulfill your obligations. You're building foundations for an outlet for your creativity.

Tuesday, November 5 (Moon in Sagittarius)   Venus moves into your first house today. You're more socially outgoing than usual, Capricorn. Your personal grace and magnetism attract others who find you appealing now. Accept the compliments, but avoid acting overly vain.

Wednesday, November 6 (Moon into Capricorn, 4:44 p.m.)   Service to others is the theme of the day. You offer advice and support. Be sympathetic and kind, generous and tolerant. Diplomacy wins the way. Help others, but dance to your own tune.

Thursday, November 7 (Moon in Capricorn)   Jupiter goes direct in your seventh house today. That's good news. Now you have an opportunity to expand whatever you're doing related to a contract or partnership. You see the big picture. You also can improve a relationship, either a business or personal one.

Friday, November 8 (Moon into Aquarius, 6:31 p.m.)   It's a number 8 day, your power day. Focus on a power play. Business dealings go well. You can go far with your plans and achieve financial success. You're playing with power, so be careful not to hurt others. It's a good day to buy a lotto ticket.

Saturday, November 9 (Moon in Aquarius)   The moon is in your second house today. You can expect an emotional reaction related to money and finances. Money and material goods are important to you now and give you a sense of security. You identify emotionally with your possessions or whatever you value. Watch your spending. Look at your priorities in handling your income.

Sunday, November 10 (Moon into Pisces, 9:37 p.m.)
Mercury goes direct in your eleventh house today. That means any confusion, miscommunication, and delays that you've been experiencing recede into the past. Things go more smoothly, especially related to dealings with friends, associates, or a group. You can move ahead with your wishes and dreams.

Monday, November 11 (Moon in Pisces) The moon is in your third house today. Your mental abilities are strong now, and you have an emotional need to reinvigorate your studies, especially regarding matters of the past. You're attracted to historical or archaeological studies. You write from a deep place; it's a good day for journaling. Female relatives play a role.

Tuesday, November 12 (Moon in Pisces) Under the influence of the Pisces moon, your imagination is highlighted. You respond emotionally to whatever is happening. Keep track of your dreams, including your daydreams. Ideas are ripe. Turn inward for inspiration, universal knowledge, and eternal truths.

Wednesday, November 13 (Moon into Aries, 2:40 a.m.) Neptune goes direct in your third house today. There could be some difficulties in dealing with neighbors, siblings, or other family members. Something secretive and deceptive is going on, and it could relate to the past. Move with care when discussing your concerns. Be aware that you could be overanalyzing whatever is going on.

Thursday, November 14 (Moon in Aries)   The moon is in your fourth house today. You're dealing with your domestic life and the foundations of who you are. Spend time at home with family and other loved ones. Take the day off, if possible, or work at home. It's a good day to handle repairs on your house. Find some time for meditation.

Friday, November 15 (Moon into Taurus, 9:50 a.m.) Service to others is the theme of the day. Be sympathetic and kind, generous and tolerant. Do a good deed for someone. Visit someone who is ill or in need of help. An adjustment in your domestic life may be necessary now.

Saturday, November 16 (Moon in Taurus)   The moon is in your fifth house today, Capricorn. You feel strongly attached to loved ones and protective of children. Your emotions tend to overpower your intellect. You're also emotionally in touch with your creative side now. Sex for pleasure is highlighted.

Sunday, November 17 (Moon into Gemini, 7:08 p.m.) There's a full moon in your fifth house. That means you find new opportunities for pursuing a creative project. Your emotions are enhanced, and you come on strong in a romantic relationship. Express your joy. Seek pleasure and fun. Avoid any tendency to become overbearing.

Monday, November 18 (Moon in Gemini)   The moon is in your sixth house today. It's a service-oriented day. Help others, but be careful not to fall into a martyr syndrome. Don't let your fears hold you back. Attend to details related to your health. Make a doctor or dentist appointment.

Tuesday, November 19 (Moon in Gemini) Under the influence of the Gemini moon, you're feeling restless and impatient. You get your ideas across and are busy sending messages or talking on the phone. You're looking for intellectual stimulation. However, you tend to analyze and rationalize too much today.

Wednesday, November 20 (Moon into Cancer, 6:24 a.m.) Use your intuition to get a sense of the day. Don't make waves. Don't rush or show resentment; let things develop. The spotlight is on cooperation. Show your appreciation to others.

Thursday, November 21 (Moon in Cancer) The moon is in your seventh house today. You feel a strong desire to work with a partner now. You don't feel complete unless you and your partner or spouse are in tune. Avoid conflicts; go with the flow.

Friday, November 22 (Moon into Leo, 6:57 p.m.) Your organizational skills are highlighted. Control your impulses. Self-discipline and structure are key. Fulfill your obligations. Maintain emotional balance. You're building foundations for an outlet for your creativity.

Saturday, November 23 (Moon in Leo) With the moon in your eighth house today, you explore the deeper mysteries of life. Past lives and life after death are on your radar. Your psychic abilities are highlighted. Issues of the day also could include matters related to shared income or belongings. Avoid any tendency toward selfishness.

Sunday, November 24 (Moon in Leo)   You're creative and passionate today, impulsive and honest. Romance feels majestic. Dress boldly; showmanship is emphasized. You're at center stage. Focus on advertising, publicity, and publicizing yourself.

Monday, November 25 (Moon into Virgo, 7:11 a.m.) It's a number 7 day. You work best on your own. Secrets, intrigue, confidential information play a role. You investigate, analyze, or simply observe what's going on now. You quickly come to a conclusion and wonder why others don't see what you see. You detect deception and recognize insincerity with ease. Maintain your emotional balance.

Tuesday, November 26 (Moon in Virgo)   The moon is in your ninth house today. You're a dreamer and a thinker, and you yearn for new experiences. It's a great time to sign up for a workshop or seminar on a subject of interest. You could also follow your wanderlust and plan a long journey. Study and investigate possible destinations and sites along the way.

Wednesday, November 27 (Moon into Libra, 5 p.m.) It's a number 9 day. Use the day for reflection, expansion, and concluding projects. Take an inventory on where things are going in your life. Make room for something new, but don't start anything until tomorrow.

Thursday, November 28 (Moon in Libra)   Under the influence of the Libra moon, romance is highlighted. Relationship issues figure prominently in your day. Your creativity, personal grace, and magnetism are emphasized. You're also looking for balance as you fine-tune a love relationship. Happy Thanksgiving.

Friday, November 29 (Moon into Scorpio, 11:04 p.m.)   The spotlight is on cooperation. Don't make waves. Don't rush or show resentment; let things develop. Show your appreciation to others. Use your intuition to get a sense of the day.

Saturday, November 30 (Moon in Scorpio)   The moon is in your eleventh house today. You have deeper contact with friends. You find strength in numbers and meaning through friends and groups. You work for the common good. Sagittarius and Aries play a role in your day.

DECEMBER 2013

Sunday, December 1 (Moon in Scorpio)   The moon is in your eleventh house today. Even though it's Sunday, your attention is squarely focused on professional matters. You feel very strongly about things happening in the workplace, and you benefit from the changes or new activity. You feel close to certain people, but be careful to keep your personal and business life separate.

Monday, December 2 (Moon into Sagittarius, 1:32 a.m.) There's a new moon in your twelfth house today. It's a good day to stay out of sight and work behind the scenes. You find new opportunities now, but it's best to keep them to yourself for the time being. Take time to reflect and meditate. Pay attention to synchronicities, and see where they lead you.

Tuesday, December 3 (Moon in Sagittarius) Yesterday's energy flows into your Tuesday. You might feel a need to withdraw today and work on your own. Things concerning the past and your childhood play a role. You hide your emotions and moodiness. Take time to reflect and meditate.

Wednesday, December 4 (Moon into Capricorn, 1:51 a.m.) Mercury moves into your twelfth house today. It's a great day for journaling and spending time on your own. You tend to be secretive about your thoughts now. Your decisions are heavily influenced by your feelings. Look for ways to expand whatever you're doing.

Thursday, December 5 (Moon in Capricorn) The moon is on your ascendant today, and that makes you more appealing to the public. You're physically vital, and relations with the opposite sex go well. Your appearance and personality shine. Your feelings and thoughts are aligned, and you're recharged for the rest of the month.

Friday, December 6 (Moon into Aquarius, 1:55 a.m.) It's a number 7 day, your mystery day. You're a searcher and a seeker. Secrets, intrigue, confidential information play a role. You investigate, analyze, or simply observe what's going on now. You quickly come to a conclusion and wonder why others don't see what you see. You detect deception and recognize insincerity with ease.

Saturday, December 7 (Moon in Aquarius) Mars moves into your ninth house today. You're adventurous now and could pursue an interest in long-distance travel, sports, and outdoor activities. You forcefully and convincingly espouse your ideas. You aggressively pursue higher-education opportunities.

Sunday, December 8 (Moon into Pisces, 3:35 a.m.) Use the day for reflection, expansion, and concluding projects. Take an inventory on where things are going in your life. Make room for something new, but don't start anything until tomorrow. Romance feels majestic. Dress boldly; showmanship is emphasized.

Monday, December 9 (Moon in Pisces) The moon is in your third house today. You're busy interacting with neighbors, relatives, or siblings in a social gathering. You get your ideas across, but try not to get too emotional. A female relative plays an important role.

Tuesday, December 10 (Moon into Aries, 8:06 a.m.) Partnerships are highlighted. Use your intuition to get a sense of your day, and focus on relationships. Be kind and understanding. The spotlight is on cooperation. Emotions and your sensitivity play a role.

Wednesday, December 11 (Moon in Aries)   With the moon in your fourth house, it's a good day to stick close to home and spend time with loved ones. Your home life and roots are important now. It's all about your foundations, the person you are, and the one you are becoming.

Thursday, December 12 (Moon into Taurus, 3:41 p.m.)   It's a number 4 day, and it's time to get focused. Persevere to get things done today, and don't get sloppy. Tear down the old in order to rebuild. Be methodical and thorough, and stay on task. Revise and rewrite.

Friday, December 13 (Moon in Taurus)   The moon is in your fifth house today. It's a great day for pursuing a romance. There's greater emotional depth in whatever you pursue. Be yourself, be emotionally honest. You're creative now and have the ability to tap deeply into the collective unconscious. Children and pets could play a role.

Saturday, December 14 (Moon in Taurus)   Under the influence of the Taurus moon, it's a good day to cultivate new ideas. But make sure that they're down to earth. Your senses are highly developed and attuned today. You're sensual and opinionated. Again, avoid any urge to act in a stubborn manner. Health and physical activity are highlighted.

Sunday, December 15 (Moon into Gemini, 1:41 a.m.) It's another mystery day, Capricorn. Secrets, intrigue, confidential information play a role. Investigate activities taking place behind closed doors. You work best on your own today. Keep your own counsel. Knowledge is essential to success. Gather information, but don't make any absolute decisions until tomorrow.

Monday, December 16 (Moon in Gemini)   The moon is in your sixth house today. It's a service day. You improve, edit, and refine the work of others. Help them, but don't deny your own needs. It's a good day to clarify any health or work issues. It's best if you follow a regular schedule now.

Tuesday, December 17 (Moon into Cancer, 1:17 p.m.)   With Uranus going direct in your fourth house today, you feel a strong need to spend time working on a home-repair project or with family members. Alternately, you could be dealing with parents now. Meanwhile, there's a full moon in your sixth house, which suggests that you reap what you've sown related all that you've done to help others.

Wednesday, December 18 (Moon in Cancer)   The moon is in your seventh house today. Relationships take on more importance. You comprehend the nuances of a situation, but it's difficult to go with the flow. You might have trouble now getting in touch with your own feelings. Alternately, a legal matter comes to your attention.

Thursday, December 19 (Moon in Cancer)   Under the influence of the Cancer moon, it's a good day to beautify your home or take care of home repairs. But also tend to loved ones, do something with your children or sweetheart. You're sensitive to other people's moods. It's best to keep things to yourself to avoid arguments.

Friday, December 20 (Moon into Leo, 1:48 a.m.) It's a number 3 day. Your attitude determines everything today. Spread your good news. Take time to relax, enjoy yourself, recharge your batteries. Have fun in preparation for tomorrow's discipline and focus.

Saturday, December 21 (Moon in Leo) Venus goes retrograde in your first house, where it stays until January 31. There could be some confusion related to a matter from the past. Siblings, other relatives, or neighbors might misunderstand your efforts to share your knowledge. As a result, you tend to pull back and work on your own.

Sunday, December 22 (Moon into Virgo, 2:20 p.m.) It's a number 5 day. Freedom of thought and action is key now. Variety is the spice of life. Take risks; experiment. Approach the day with an unconventional mindset. You're versatile and changeable, Capricorn.

Monday, December 23 (Moon in Virgo) The moon is in your ninth house today, the home of higher learning. You're considering ideas now on matters such as philosophy or religion, the law or publishing. You also have a strong interest in foreign travel or a foreign nation. Break away from your routine or the usual way you think about things. You can create positive change through your ideas, especially if you express them forcefully.

Tuesday, December 24 (Moon in Virgo)   Mercury moves into your first house today. You communicate well and easily get your ideas across. Your mind is quick and witty, and you smoothly adapt to changing circumstances.

Wednesday, December 25 (Moon into Libra, 1:18 a.m.)   It's a number 8 day, your power day. You have a chance to expand, to gain recognition, fame, power. Be courageous. Be yourself; be honest. You're playing with power, so be careful not to hurt others. Merry Christmas, Capricorn.

Thursday, December 26 (Moon in Libra)   The moon is in your tenth house today. New opportunities arise related to your career. Professional concerns are on your mind as you pursue an elevation of prestige, a raise, or a promotion. You get along well with bosses and peers, but make sure that you don't get overly emotional in public.

Friday, December 27 (Moon into Scorpio, 8:59 a.m.) It's a number 1 day, so you're at the top of your cycle, Capricorn. Express your opinions dynamically. Get out and meet new people, have new experiences, do something you've never done before. Refuse to deal with people who have closed minds. In romance a flirtation turns more serious, if that's what you want.

Saturday, December 28 (Moon in Scorpio)   With the moon in your eleventh house today, friends play an important role. You find strength in numbers and meaning through friends and groups. Focus on your

223

wishes and dreams. Examine your overall goals. Those goals should be an expression of who you are.

Sunday, December 29 (Moon into Sagittarius, 12:38 p.m.)   It's a number 3 day. You can influence people now with your upbeat attitude. Your charm and wit are appreciated. Your attitude determines everything. Spread your good news. Ease up on routines, and remain flexible.

Monday, December 30 (Moon in Sagittarius)   The moon is in your twelfth house today. It's a great day for a mystical or spiritual discipline. Your intuition is heightened. Unconscious attitudes can be difficult now. So can relations with women. Keep your feelings secret. Follow your intuition.

Tuesday, December 31 (Moon into Capricorn, 1:02 p.m.)   It's a number 5 day. That means travel and variety are highlighted. You're seeking new horizons. Promote new ideas, follow your curiosity. Look for adventure. You're versatile and changeable. Be careful not to spread out and diversify too much.

HAPPY NEW YEAR!

JANUARY 2014

Wednesday, January 1 (Moon in Capricorn) There's a new moon in your first house today and five planets in Capricorn. Look for new opportunities related to your willingness to change and adjust to new circumstances and feelings toward others. It's a great day for starting something new. But stay grounded, Capricorn. Be yourself. Be emotionally honest, and stay in control of your emotions. Your intellect is strong, but so are your emotions. Your feelings and thoughts are aligned.

Thursday, January 2 (Moon into Aquarius, 12:04 p.m.) You're diplomatic today and capable of fixing whatever has gone wrong. Use your intuition to get a sense of the day. Take time again to consider the direction you're headed and your motivation for continuing on this path.

Friday, January 3 (Moon in Aquarius) The moon is in your second house today. Money and material goods are important to you and give you a sense of security, Capricorn. You feel best when surrounded by familiar objects, especially in your home environment. It's not the objects themselves that are important, but the feelings and memories you associate with them. Look at your priorities in handling your income.

Saturday, January 4 (Moon into Pisces, 11:59 a.m.) It's a number 4 day, and that means the emphasis today is on your organizational skills. In romance your persistence pays off. You're building a foundation for the future. Control your impulses to wander off to another task; fulfill your obligations. You can overcome bureaucratic red tape.

Sunday, January 5 (Moon in Pisces) The moon is in your third house today. It's a good time for expressing yourself through writing. Make use of your imagination. Take what you know, and share it. As you go about your everyday life, stay grounded and remain sympathetic to others.

Monday, January 6 (Moon into Aries, 2:46 p.m.)
Service to others is the theme of the day. You offer advice and support. Be sympathetic and kind, generous and tolerant. Focus on making people happy. Diplomacy wins the way.

Tuesday, January 7 (Moon in Aries)   The moon is in your fourth house today. Spend time with your family and other loved ones. Stick close to home, if possible. It's a good day to retreat to a private place to meditate. You're dealing with the foundations of who you are and who you are becoming. A parent plays a role in your day.

Wednesday, January 8 (Moon into Taurus, 9:24 p.m.)
It's a number 8 day, your power day. Open your mind to a new approach that could bring in big bucks. You can go far with your plans and achieve financial success. You're playing with power today, so be careful not to hurt others.

Thursday, January 9 (Moon in Taurus)   The moon is in your fifth house today. Be yourself; be emotionally honest. In love there's greater emotional depth to a relationship now. It's a good day to take a chance, experiment. You're more protective and nurturing toward children.

Friday, January 10 (Moon in Taurus) Under the influence of the Taurus moon, your health and physical activity are highlighted. Go hiking; get out in nature. It's a good time for doing practical things, cultivating ideas. Try to avoid stubborn behavior when others question your actions. You could be somewhat possessive now. While you maintain a common-sense, down-to-earth perspective on life, Capricorn, you also long for the good life with its material blessings.

Saturday, January 11 (Moon into Gemini, 7:26 a.m.) Mercury enters your second house today. You tend to express yourself with a dramatic flair now. It's a good day for teaching or acting. You're grounded and also mentally stimulated by challenges, especially involving a writing project. Children play a role in your day.

Sunday, January 12 (Moon in Gemini) With the moon in your sixth house today, it's a service day. Help others, but don't deny your own needs. It's a good day to clarify any health or work issues. It's best if you follow a regular schedule now.

Monday, January 13 (Moon into Cancer, 7:25 p.m.) It's a number 4 day. Tear down the old in order to rebuild. Be methodical and thorough. Hard work is called for. Be practical with your money. You may feel inhibited in showing affection. Do things like cleaning your closet or clearing out your garage.

Tuesday, January 14 (Moon in Cancer) The moon is in your seventh house today. You get along well with others. You can fit in just about anywhere.

Loved ones and partners are more important than usual. But be careful that others don't manipulate your feelings.

Wednesday, January 15 (Moon in Cancer)   There's a full moon in your seventh house today with Saturn forming a beneficial angle. You reap what you've sown related to partnerships, either business or personal. You take a more serious approach to your relationship with a partner, especially if you are entering a new venture or adventure.

Thursday, January 16 (Moon into Leo, 8:01 a.m.) It's a number 7 day, your mystery day. You launch a new journey into the unknown. You seek information, knowledge, wisdom. You work best on your own today. You investigate, analyze, or simply observe what's going on now. You quickly come to a conclusion and wonder why others don't see what you see.

Friday, January 17 (Moon in Leo)   The moon is in your eighth house today. Your experiences are more intense than usual. You have a strong sense of duty and feel obligated to fulfill your promises. Security is an important issue with you right now, Capricorn. You could find yourself managing or controlling someone else's assets.

Saturday, January 18 (Moon into Virgo, 8:25 p.m.) It's a number 9 day. Visualize for the future. Set your goals, then make them so. Strive for universal appeal; you're up to the challenge. Complete a project and get ready for something new that's coming up soon.

Sunday, January 19 (Moon in Virgo) The moon is in your ninth house today. That means it's a good time to start thinking about a long trip. Make your plans now. You're feeling restless. It's also a good time to explore ideas, philosophies, mythology. Higher education and the higher mind are highlighted. You're a dreamer and thinker.

Monday, January 20 (Moon in Virgo) Under the influence of the Virgo moon, it's a good time to take care of details, especially related to a contract or partnership. Stop worrying and fretting. Dig deep for information. Take time to write in a journal. You write from a deep place with lots of details and colorful descriptions. Remember to exercise and watch your diet.

Tuesday, January 21 (Moon into Libra, 7:45 a.m.) It's a number 3 day. You have a strong sense of duty and feel obligated to fulfill your promises, Capricorn. You're warm and receptive to what others say. Your imagination is keen now. You're curious and inventive. Enjoy the harmony, beauty, and pleasures of life.

Wednesday, January 22 (Moon in Libra) The moon is in your tenth house today, and professional concerns are on your mind. You could be involved in a power struggle. Remain responsive to the needs and moods of others around you. Try to stay grounded, Capricorn, and keep everyone around you in balance. Avoid making any emotional displays in public now.

Thursday, January 23 (Moon into Scorpio, 4:45 p.m.) It's a number 5 day, and that means freedom of thought and action is key today. It's a good time to pursue self-employment. You're courageous and adaptable. Travel and adventure are highlighted, so is meeting new people. You're versatile, changeable, and willing to let go of old structures and get a new point of view.

Friday, January 24 (Moon in Scorpio)   The moon is in your eleventh house today. You find strength in numbers and meaning through friends and groups. You work for the common good, but keep an eye on your own wishes and dreams. Social consciousness plays a role.

Saturday, January 25 (Moon into Sagittarius, 10:14 p.m.)   You launch a journey into the unknown and pursue a mystery today, Capricorn. Dig deep, and look behind closed doors. Confidential information and secrets are involved. Knowledge is essential to success. Go with the flow. Maintain your emotional balance, and don't make any absolute decisions until tomorrow.

Sunday, January 26 (Moon in Sagittarius)   With the moon in your twelfth house today, you may feel like withdrawing and remaining behind the scenes. You could be dealing with a matter from your childhood. Be aware of hidden enemies, but think carefully before you act. There's a tendency now to undo all the positive actions you've taken.

Monday, January 27 (Moon in Sagittarius)   Under the influence of the Sag moon, you see the big picture today, not just the details. You're restless and looking for ways to expand whatever you're doing, especially if it relates to travel or higher education. Worldviews are emphasized. Don't limit yourself. Keep track of your dreams, including your daydreams. Ideas are ripe.

Tuesday, January 28 (Moon into Capricorn, 12:05 a.m.) It's a number 1 day. You're inventive and make connections that others overlook. You're determined and courageous today. Stress originality. In romance something new is developing. A flirtation turns more serious. Explore, discover, create.

Wednesday, January 29 (Moon into Aquarius, 11:33 p.m.) The moon is in your second house. Finances and money issue take center stage now, Capricorn. Collect what's owed to you, and pay off what's due. You identify emotionally with your possessions or whatever you value. Watch your spending. You feel best when surrounded by familiar objects, especially in your home environment.

Thursday, January 30 (Moon in Aquarius) There's a new moon in your second house today, and that indicates a new opportunity related to your everyday world, family, or neighbors. Maybe you make an investment that pays off. With Uranus forming a beneficial angle, whatever happens shakes you out of a rut. You embrace what's new and different.

Friday, January 31 (Moon into Pisces, 10:45 p.m.) Mercury moves into your third house today. Your mind is highly stimulated, and you tend to jump from one thing to the next. You express yourself well. You're witty and clever and can verbally spar with anyone. You're also versatile and adaptable. With Venus going direct in your first house until March 5, personal matters need special attention. It could involve your health or how you see yourself in front of the public. Pamper yourself; buy yourself something special.

FEBRUARY 2014

Saturday, February 1 (Moon in Pisces)   The moon is in your third house today. Take what you know, and share it with others, especially family members. Be yourself, but stay in control of your emotions when communicating. You write from a deep place. It's a good day for journaling, especially about matters from the past.

Sunday, February 2 (Moon into Aries, 11:55 p.m.) It's a number 3 day, and that means you're creative and express yourself well. Your artistic talents are highlighted. Enjoy the harmony, beauty, and pleasures of life. Beautify your home. Your charm and wit are appreciated.

Monday, February 3 (Moon in Aries)   The moon is in your fourth house today. You're dealing with the foundations of who you are and who you are becoming. Retreat to a private place for meditation. It's a good day for dream recall. You feel a close tie to your roots.

Tuesday, February 4 (Moon in Aries)   It's a great day for initiating projects, launching new ideas, brainstorming. However, emotions could be volatile. You're passionate but impatient. You're extremely persuasive now, especially if you're intense about what you're doing, selling, or trying to convey.

Wednesday, February 5 (Moon into Taurus, 4:47 a.m.)   It's a number 6 day, a service day. A domestic adjustment works out for the best. You could face emotional outbursts by someone making unfair demands. Be understanding, and avoid confrontations. Help others, but dance to your own tune.

Thursday, February 6 (Moon in Taurus)   Mercury goes retrograde in your third house and stays there until February 28. That means you can expect delays and glitches related to your everyday life and your dealings with siblings, other relatives, and neighbors. You communicate what you want, but others seem to misinterpret your intentions. There also could be confusion about a matter from the past.

Friday, February 7 (Moon into Gemini, 1:45 p.m.)
It's a number 8 day. It's your power day and your day to play it your way. You can go far with your plans and achieve financial success. However, be aware that you're playing with power, so try not to hurt anyone.

Saturday, February 8 (Moon in Gemini)   The moon is in your sixth house today. People are depending on you, and that can be a burden. Keep everyone informed about what you can do for them and what you can't. Stop worrying; you're better off than you might think. You're restless and looking for change in your daily routine. A new job could be in store.

Sunday, February 9 (Moon in Gemini)   Under the influence of the Gemini moon, you're mentally quick and communicate well. You see two sides of an issue. You're feeling creative and need to express yourself in writing. A change of scenery would do you good today, possibly a short trip to visit friends or relatives.

Monday, February 10 (Moon into Cancer, 1:34 a.m.) It's a number 2 day, and that means cooperation is highlighted. Marriage and partnerships are more important than usual. Your intuition focuses on relationships. Don't make waves. Let things develop, even if someone is nagging you.

Tuesday, February 11 (Moon in Cancer)   The moon is in your seventh house today. So partnership issues are the focus of your day. A legal matter comes to your attention. Women play a prominent role. You comprehend the nuances of a situation, but it's difficult to go with the flow.

Wednesday, February 12 (Moon into Leo, 2:17 p.m.) It's a number 4 day, back to the grind. Get organized. Hard work is called for. Stay focused, and avoid wandering off task. Take care of obligations. Emphasize quality.

Thursday, February 13 (Moon in Leo)   With the moon in your eighth house, you could attract powerful people to you. Be aware that your experiences may be more intense than usual today. You could be dealing with belongings that you share with someone else. Alternately, a metaphysical subject attracts your attention. You could take an interest in what happens after death.

Friday, February 14 (Moon in Leo)   There's a full moon in your eighth house today, and you take another look at a metaphysical subject, such as life after death, reincarnation, or ghosts. You gain insight and illumination, possibly as a result of a personal experience or from news that you hear. Happy Valentine's Day!

Saturday, February 15 (Moon into Virgo, 2:27 a.m.) It's a number 7 day. That means you could be launching a journey into the unknown. Look beneath the surface for the reasons others are shifting their points of view, changing their tune. Secrets, intrigue, confidential information play a role. But don't make any final decisions on what you uncover until tomorrow. Knowledge is the key to success.

Sunday, February 16 (Moon in Virgo)   The moon is in your ninth house today. You're a dreamer and thinker. You yearn for a new experience. You may feel a need to get away now, a break from the usual routine. Foreigners or a foreign country plays a role in your day.

Monday, February 17 (Moon into Libra, 1:24 p.m.) It's a number 9 day. Visualize the future; set your goals, then make them so. Complete a project. Clear up odds and ends. Take an inventory on where things are going in your life. It's a good day to make a donation to a worthy cause.

Tuesday, February 18 (Moon in Libra)   The moon is in your tenth house today. You're thinking about your career and where it's going. You're seeking to elevate yourself through a promotion, a raise or even a pat on the back for a job well done. Your life is more public. Best to avoid mixing your personal and business lives or emotional displays in public now.

Wednesday, February 19 (Moon into Scorpio, 10:33 p.m.)   It's a number 2 day. That means cooperation and partnership are highlighted again. There's a new beginning, or a new opportunity arises. Your intuition focuses on relationships. Don't make waves. Don't rush or show resentment; let things develop.

Thursday, February 20 (Moon in Scorpio)   With the moon in your eleventh house today, friends play an important role, especially Taurus and Virgo. Take a look at your goals, and make sure that they're still an expression of who you are. You do well in a group setting. You could be dealing with an issue involving social consciousness.

Friday, February 21 (Moon in Scorpio)   Under the influence of the Scorpio moon, yesterday's energy flows into your Friday. Your emotions grow intense as you investigate an important matter. Control issues arise. Be aware of things happening in secret. Forgive and forget; try to avoid going to extremes. You're also passionate today; your sexuality is heightened.

Saturday, February 22 (Moon into Sagittarius, 5:12 a.m.) It's a number 5 day. That means it's time to shed yourself of self-imposed restrictions. Think freedom. Variety is the spice of life. Take risks; experiment. Approach the day with an unconventional mindset. Promote new ideas, and follow your curiosity.

Sunday, February 23 (Moon in Sagittarius) The moon is in your twelfth house today. Think carefully before you act. There's a tendency now to undo all the positive actions you've taken. You're more sensitive than usual, Capricorn. Avoid any self-destructive behavior. Best to back off rather than confront a suspected enemy.

Monday, February 24 (Moon into Capricorn, 8:51 a.m.) It's a number 7 day, another mystery day. Secrets, intrigue, confidential information play a role. Knowledge is essential to success. Express your desires, but avoid self-deception. Maintain your emotional balance.

Tuesday, February 25 (Moon in Capricorn) The moon is on your ascendant today. The way you see yourself now is the way others see you. Your face is in front of the public. You're recharged for the month ahead, and this makes you more appealing. Your appearance and personality shine. Your feelings and thoughts are aligned.

Wednesday, February 26 (Moon into Aquarius, 9:56 a.m.)   It's a number 9 day. That means it's time to complete a project. Clear your desk, and make room for the new, but don't start anything until tomorrow. Spend some time in deep thought. Consider how you can expand your base.

Thursday, February 27 (Moon in Aquarius)   The moon is in your second house today. You feel best when surrounded by familiar objects, your things. It's not the objects themselves that are important, but the feelings and memories you associate with them. Put off making any major purchases. You equate your financial assets with emotional security.

Friday, February 28 (Moon into Pisces, 9:53 a.m.) Mercury goes direct in your second house today. Confusion, miscommunication, and delays, especially related to your finances, recede into the past. Things move more smoothly. You're mentally alert and quick witted, and people instantly understand. You get along with others better, and you get your message across about your values or whatever you value most. Everything works better, including computers and other electronic equipment.

MARCH 2014

Saturday, March 1 (Moon in Pisces)   There's a new moon in your third house, which means new opportunities come your way related to your community, relatives, or siblings. Meanwhile Mars turns retrograde in your tenth house, where it stays until May 19. That suggests that any aggressive actions you take related to your career will be met by delays and confusion. With Neptune forming a favorable conjunction, you can move ahead on a project related to your everyday world. Conditions also turn favorable for any intellectual pursuits, such as gaming or debating.

Sunday, March 2 (Moon into Aries, 10:41 a.m.) Saturn turns retrograde in your eleventh house today, where it stays until July 20. You'll be thinking more about your wishes and dreams. Friends and associates or a group you're associated with play an important role in your day. By the time Saturn goes direct again, you should be able to better integrate your wishes and dreams into your daily life.

Monday, March 3 (Moon in Aries) With the moon in your fourth house today, it's a good day to attend to domestic matters. Spend time with your family and other loved ones. Make an effort to change a bad habit. It's best to work on your own, especially on a project to beautify your home.

Tuesday, March 4 (Moon into Taurus, 2:13 p.m.) It's a number 6 day, a service day. A domestic adjustment works out for the best. You could face emotional outbursts by someone making unfair demands. Be understanding and diplomatic. Avoid confrontations or stubborn behavior, Capricorn. Help others, but dance to your own tune.

Wednesday, March 5 (Moon in Taurus) Venus moves into your second house today, where it stays until April 5. You have a love of the better things in life and an opportunity to obtain them. You feel a strong desire to make money, but also an urge to spend it. Hold off on making any large purchases. Follow your creative and artistic endeavors; you have a good chance of making money on whatever you create.

Thursday, March 6 (Moon into Gemini, 9:39 p.m.) Jupiter goes direct in your eighth house today, which means that you have an opportunity in coming days, weeks, and months to expand your interest in metaphysical subjects, such as astrology or psychic abilities. You can expand and grow. Focus on abundance and a strong relationship with someone with whom you share resources. You're very persistent and grounded, Capricorn.

Friday, March 7 (Moon in Gemini) With the moon in your sixth house today, the emphasis turns to your daily work and service to others. Attend to all the details, and be careful not to overlook any seemingly minor matters that could take on importance. Keep up with your exercise plan, and watch your diet.

Saturday, March 8 (Moon in Gemini) Under the influence of the Gemini moon, you're mentally quick and communicate well. You see two sides of an issue. You're feeling creative and need to express yourself in writing. A change of scenery would do you good today, possibly a short trip to visit friends or relatives.

Sunday, March 9—Daylight Saving Time Begins (Moon into Cancer, 9:34 a.m.) It's a number 2 day. That means it's all about cooperation and partnerships now. You're diplomatic and capable of fixing whatever has gone wrong. You're persistent and determined to succeed, Capricorn. You're ambitious in pursuing a partnership. You excel in working with others. You're playing the role of the visionary. Be honest and open.

Monday, March 10 (Moon in Cancer)   The moon is in your seventh house today. You get along well with others. You can fit in just about anywhere. Loved ones and partners are more important than usual. But be careful that others don't manipulate your feelings.

Tuesday, March 11 (Moon into Leo, 10:10 p.m.) It's a number 4 day. Your organizational skills are highlighted. Persevere to get things done today. Control your impulses. It's not a good day for romance. Tear down the old in order to rebuild. Be methodical and thorough.

Wednesday, March 12 (Moon in Leo)   The moon is in your eighth house today. Take care of any matters related to taxes, insurance, or investments. Be aware that emotions can get intense, especially when dealing with shared resources. Metaphysics could play a role in your day. You could be dealing with a mystery of the unknown, such as what happens after death.

Thursday, March 13 (Moon in Leo)   Under the influence of the Leo moon, theatrics and drama are highlighted. You're at center stage today. You like to flaunt and celebrate. Be wild, imaginative; be the person you always imagined you might be. Play with different personae.

Friday, March 14 (Moon into Virgo, 10:18 a.m.) It's your mystery day, Capricorn. Secrets, intrigue, confidential information play a role. You're a spy for your own cause today. Knowledge is essential to success. But make sure that you see things as they are, not as you wish them to be. Maintain your emotional balance. Your challenge is to be independent without feeling isolated.

Saturday, March 15 (Moon in Virgo)   The moon is in your ninth house today. You're a dreamer and thinker. You may feel a need to get away now, a break from the usual routine. You yearn for a new experience. Plan a long trip. Sign up for a workshop or seminar. A foreigner or a foreign country plays a role.

Sunday, March 16 (Moon into Libra, 8:46 p.m.) The moon moves into your tenth house today. You can create positive change through your ideas. You guide others in their intellectual development.

Monday, March 17 (Moon in Libra)   Mercury moves into your third house today. Your mind is highly stimulated, and you tend to jump from one thing to the next. You express yourself well. You're witty and clever and can verbally spar with anyone. You're also versatile and adaptable.

Tuesday, March 18 (Moon in Libra)   The moon is in your tenth house today. Professional concerns are the focus of the day. You gain an elevation of prestige, possibly a raise or promotion. You get along well with others in the workplace. Your life is more public, so avoid emotional displays.

Wednesday, March 19 (Moon into Scorpio, 5:14 a.m.) It's a number 3 day. That means you communicate well. Your attitude determines everything today. Spread your good news. Ease up on routines. Your charm and wit are appreciated. Play your hunches. But also take time to relax and recharge your batteries.

Thursday, March 20 (Moon in Scorpio) The moon is in your eleventh house today. Group activities work in your favor now, even if you're a nonjoiner. You assist the group, and maybe to your surprise the group helps you in return. Friends also play an important role. Focus on your wishes and dreams, but make sure that your goals remain an expression of who you really are.

Friday, March 21 (Moon into Sagittarius, 11:39 a.m.) It's a number 5 day. Change and variety are highlighted. Think freedom, no restrictions. Release old structures; get a new point of view. It's a good day to take a risk, experiment. Promote new ideas. Find a new outlook that fits current circumstances and what you know now.

Saturday, March 22 (Moon in Sagittarius) The moon is in your twelfth house today. Take time to reflect and meditate. Think carefully before you act.

There's a tendency now to undo all the positive actions you've taken. Avoid any self-destructive behavior. Be aware of hidden enemies.

Sunday, March 23 (Moon into Capricorn, 4:04 p.m.)
It's a number 7 day, a mystery day. You launch a journey into the unknown. You're a searcher and seeker of truth. Knowledge is essential to success. Gather information, but don't make any absolute decisions until tomorrow. Go with the flow.

Monday, March 24 (Moon in Capricorn) With the moon in your first house today, you're sensitive to other people's feelings. You may feel moody one moment, happy the next, then withdrawn and sad. It's all about your health and emotional self: how you feel and how you feel about yourself. Your feelings and thoughts are aligned.

Tuesday, March 25 (Moon into Aquarius, 6:40 p.m.)
It's a number 9 day. Finish the day by wrapping up a project and preparing for something new. Take time to reflect on everything that's been going on. Look for a way to expand your horizons, but don't start anything new until tomorrow.

Wednesday, March 26 (Moon in Aquarius) The moon is in your second house today. It's a good day to catch up on your bills and take a look at your financial needs. You find emotional security in your assets and possessions. It's the not the objects themselves that are important. Rather it's the memories and feelings you associate with them.

Thursday, March 27 (Moon into Pisces, 8:12 p.m.)
It's a number 2 day. That means that cooperation and partnership are highlighted again. Your intuition focuses on relationships. Don't make waves. Don't rush or show resentment; let things develop.

Friday, March 28 (Moon in Pisces)   The moon is in your third house today. It's a good day to take a short trip to visit siblings or other relatives. However, stay in control of your emotions, especially when matters from the past arise. A female relative or neighbor plays a role now.

Saturday, March 29 (Moon into Aries, 9:55 p.m.)
It's a number 4 day. That means you're building foundations for an outlet for your creativity. Emphasize quality related to whatever you're working on. Persevere to get things done today. Tear down the old in order to rebuild, but do so carefully. Avoid reckless behavior.

Sunday, March 30 (Moon in Aries)   There's a new moon in your fourth house today. New opportunities come your way now related to your home. It's a good time to start a home-based business or a new project to beautify your surroundings. However, with Uranus closely conjunct, you might encounter sudden and unexpected changes in your plans. The challenge for you is to avoid getting overly concerned about any chaos in your domestic scene.

Monday, March 31 (Moon in Aries)   You feel close to your roots now. Spend time with your family and loved ones today. Stick close to home, if possible. A parent plays a role. It's a good day to work on a home-repair project.

APRIL 2014

Tuesday, April 1 (Moon into Taurus, 1:21 a.m.) It's a number 4 day, and that means the emphasis today is on your organizational skills. In romance your persistence pays off. You're building a foundation for the future. Control your impulses to wander off to another task; fulfill your obligations. You can overcome bureaucratic red tape.

Wednesday, April 2 (Moon in Taurus) The moon is in your sixth house today. It's a service-oriented day. You improve, edit, and refine the work of others. Visit someone who is sick. It's a good day to clarify any health or work issues. It's best if you follow a regular schedule now.

Thursday, April 3 (Moon into Gemini, 7:49 a.m.) It's a number 6 day, and service to others is the theme. It's time to be diplomatic. Be sympathetic and kind, generous and tolerant. Focus on making people happy. Your life is more public today. You're more responsive to the needs and moods of a group.

Friday, April 4 (Moon in Gemini) The moon is in your seventh house today. The focus turns to relationships, business and personal ones. You get along well with others, and you get a fresh start. You can fit in just about anywhere. Loved ones and partners are more important than usual. Women play a prominent role.

Saturday, April 5 (Moon into Cancer, 5:40 p.m.) Venus moves into your third house today, where it stays until May 9. That means you get along well with siblings and other family members. You feel strongly connected with your neighborhood or community. You use your mental abilities to solve any problems that come up.

Sunday, April 6 (Moon in Cancer)   Baseball season has finally started. Get out to a game or watch one on TV. Even better, get the neighbors out for your own game. If you don't like baseball, go for a hike — get out and enjoy the day.

Monday, April 7 (Moon in Cancer)   Mercury moves into your fourth house today and stays there until April 24. There's lots of studying going on in the home now. At this rate you could get a degree without leaving home, Capricorn! You exchange ideas with family members, friends, or visitors. You gain energy and support from your family and the home scene.

Tuesday, April 8 (Moon into Leo, 5:51 a.m.)   It's a number 2 day. Help comes through friends. A partner or lover plays a role. Focus on your direction, your motivation. Where are you going and why? The spotlight is on cooperation. Show your appreciation to others.

Wednesday, April 9 (Moon in Leo)   The moon is in your eighth house today. You can expect high emotions regarding a troubling matter, especially if it deals with shared belongings. You dig deep, seeking the details. A mortgage, insurance, or investments could play a role. Alternately, you could be looking into a metaphysical subject, such as life after death.

Thursday, April 10 (Moon into Virgo, 6:08 p.m.) It's a number 4 day. Your organizational skills are highlighted. Try not to wander off task. Emphasize quality; you're building a creative foundation for your future. Tear down the old in order to rebuild. Be methodical and thorough.

Friday, April 11 (Moon in Virgo) The moon is in your ninth house today. Your mind is active, and you yearn for new experiences, a break from the routine, a change from the status quo. Your thoughts run wild. You're a dreamer and thinker, and your thoughts tend to rattle the status quo. You jump easily from one idea to another.

Saturday, April 12 (Moon in Virgo) Under the influence of the Virgo moon, it's a good time to take care of details, especially related to a contract or partnership. Stop worrying and fretting. Dig deep for information. Take time to write in a journal. You write from a deep place with lots of details and colorful descriptions. Remember to exercise and watch your diet.

Sunday, April 13 (Moon into Libra, 4:34 a.m.) It's a number 7 day. You launch a journey into the unknown and pursue a mystery. Dig deep, and look behind closed doors. Confidential information is involved. You're a spy for your own cause today. Knowledge is essential to success. It's a good day to work on your own.

Monday, April 14 (Moon in Libra)   Pluto goes retrograde in your first house today, where it stays until September 22. Take a deep look at your personal situation, especially your emotions. The energy is turned inward now. You're dealing more with your self-awareness and emotional life. It's not a good time to make any major life-changing decisions. Matters related to your health could play a role. But look within for answers rather than turning to others.

Tuesday, April 15 (Moon into Scorpio, 12:21 p.m.) There's a lunar eclipse in Libra, your tenth house, today. You gain insight into a matter involving your career or fellow workers. It could relate to your interest in a promotion. You seek more recognition. With Mars forming a positive angle, whatever happens provides you with new energy that will work to your advantage.

Wednesday, April 16 (Moon in Scorpio)   With the moon in your eleventh house today, you gain through your business and personal contacts. Friends play an important role in your day. Focus on your wishes and dreams. Examine your overall goals. Those goals should be an expression of who you are.

Thursday, April 17 (Moon into Sagittarius, 5:44 p.m.)   It's a number 2 day. Yesterday's energy flows into your Thursday. Marriage or a partnership plays a key role. The spotlight is on cooperation. Use your intuition to get a sense of the day.

Friday, April 18 (Moon in Sagittarius)   The moon is in your twelfth house today. Think carefully before you act, Capricorn. Stay grounded. There's a tendency now to undo all the positive actions you've taken. Avoid any self-destructive behavior. It's best to work behind the scenes and stay out of the public view. Be aware of hidden enemies.

Saturday, April 19 (Moon into Capricorn, 9:29 p.m.) It's a number 4 day. Tear down the old in order to re-build. Be methodical and thorough. Hard work is called for. Be practical with your money. You may feel inhibited in showing affection. Do things like cleaning your closet or clearing out the attic or garage.

Sunday, April 20 (Moon in Capricorn)   With the moon in your first house today, your feelings and thoughts are aligned. It's all about your health and emotional self: how you feel and how you feel about yourself. You are sensitive and responsive regarding the needs of others, so you are easily influenced by those around you.

Monday, April 21 (Moon in Capricorn)   Under the influence of the Capricorn moon, your ambition and drive to succeed are highlighted. Your responsibilities increase. You may feel stressed, overworked. Don't ignore your exercise routine. Authority figures and elderly people play a role.

Tuesday, April 22 (Moon into Aquarius, 12:19 a.m.)
It's your mystery day, Capricorn. You're launching a journey into the unknown. Knowledge is essential to success. You're a spy for your own cause today. Go with the flow. Maintain your emotional balance, and don't make any absolute decisions until tomorrow.

Wednesday, April 23 (Moon in Aquarius)   Mercury moves into your fifth house today. You tend to express yourself with a dramatic flair. It's a good day for teaching or acting. You're grounded and also mentally stimulated by challenges, especially involving a writing project. Children play a role in your day.

Thursday, April 24 (Moon into Pisces, 2:56 a.m.)
It's a number 9 day. Complete a project. Clear up odds and ends. Take an inventory on where things are going in your life. Make room for something new, but don't start anything today.

Friday, April 25 (Moon in Pisces)   The moon is in your third house today. Your communications with others are subjective. Take what you know, and share it, but control your emotions. That's especially true when dealing with siblings, other relatives, or neighbors. Your thinking is unduly influenced by things of the past.

Saturday, April 26 (Moon into Aries, 6:02 a.m.)
Cooperation is highlighted; you work well with others. Your intuition focuses on relationships, either a new one that's developing or a current one. Don't make

waves. Don't rush or show resentment; let things develop. Show your appreciation to others.

Sunday, April 27 (Moon in Aries) The moon is in your fourth house today. Spend time with your family and other loved ones. Stick close to home. A parent could be involved in your day. You feel close to your roots. See if you can remember a dream from last night.

Monday, April 28 (Moon into Taurus, 10:24 a.m.) It's a number 4 day. That means the emphasis today is on your organizational skills. In romance your persistence pays off. You're building a foundation for the future. Control your impulses to wander; fulfill your obligations. You could find missing papers now.

Tuesday, April 29 (Moon in Taurus) There's a solar eclipse in your fifth house today. That means new opportunities come your way related to a creative project. A romance could play a role. Whatever is coming will benefit you, especially if you keep control of your emotions. With Mercury forming a favorable angle, you communicate your ideas well, especially about how you can help others. You could also be resolving a health issue.

Wednesday, April 30 (Moon into Gemini, 4:56 p.m.) It's a number 6 day, a service day. A domestic adjustment works out for the best, Capricorn. You could face emotional outbursts by someone making unfair demands. Be understanding and diplomatic. Avoid confrontations or stubborn behavior. Help others, but dance to your own tune.

Thursday, May 1 (Moon in Gemini)   With the moon in your sixth house today, the emphasis turns to your daily work and helping others. Attend to details, and be careful not to overlook any seemingly minor matters that could take on importance. Keep up with your exercise plan, and watch your diet.

Friday, May 2 (Moon in Gemini)   Venus moves into your fourth house today. There's lots of love and affection in the home. It's a great time to beautify your home. Buy something nice for your house, change the décor, or just add a bouquet of flowers. You feel close to your roots and family members.

Saturday, May 3 (Moon into Cancer, 2:13 a.m.) It's your mystery day, Capricorn. Gather information, but don't make any absolute decisions until tomorrow. Go with the flow. Maintain your emotional balance, and avoid confusion and conflict.

Sunday, May 4 (Moon in Cancer)   The moon is in your seventh house today. The focus turns to relationships, business and personal ones. You get along well with others. You can fit in just about anywhere. Loved ones and partners are more important than usual. A legal matter comes to your attention; it could be a marriage.

Monday, May 5 (Moon into Leo, 1:56 p.m.)   It's a number 9 day. That means it's time to complete a project. Clear your desk, and make room for the new, but don't start anything until tomorrow. Spend some time in deep thought. Consider how you can expand your base.

Tuesday, May 6 (Moon in Leo)   The moon is in your eighth house today. You could be pursuing an interest in a metaphysical subject, such as life after death or past lives. Your experiences are more intense than usual. Sex, death, rebirth, rituals, and relationships all could play a role. It's a good time to get involved in a cause aimed at improving living conditions for large numbers of people.

Wednesday, May 7 (Moon in Leo)   Mercury moves into your sixth house. There's a lot of communication back and forth with coworkers. You could be providing assistance to others and explaining what they need to do. You also might be talking about a health issue this month. Your personal health occupies your attention. Make a doctor or dentist appointment.

Thursday, May 8 (Moon into Virgo, 2:25 a.m.)   As yesterday, you communicate well. You get your ideas across. Your attitude determines everything today. Spread your good news. Ease up on routines. Your charm and wit are appreciated. Play your hunches. But also take time to relax and recharge your batteries.

Friday, May 9 (Moon in Virgo)   The moon is in your ninth house today. You're feeling restless and yearning for a new experience. Plan a long trip, or sign up for a workshop or seminar on a topic that interests you. You could be attracted to mythology, philosophy, or religion. A foreign-born person or foreign land might play a role.

Saturday, May 10 (Moon into Libra, 1:20 p.m.)
It's a number 5 day. A change of scenery would work to your advantage, Capricorn. You could be moving to a new location. You're seeking new horizons, travel and adventure. Promote new ideas; follow your curiosity. You're versatile, changeable. Be careful not to spread out and diversify too much.

Sunday, May 11 (Moon in Libra)   The moon is in your tenth house today. Your life is more public. You tend to be more emotional in the workplace. But avoid emotional displays in public. You're more responsive to the needs and moods of a group and of the public in general. Business dealings are highlighted.

Monday, May 12 (Moon into Scorpio, 9:08 p.m.)
It's a number 7 day. You could be venturing into the unknown today. You investigate, analyze, or simply observe what's going on now. You quickly come to a conclusion and wonder why others don't see what you see. You detect deception and recognize insincerity with ease. Knowledge is essential to success. Avoid confusion and conflicts.

Tuesday, May 13 (Moon in Scorpio)   The moon is in your eleventh house, Capricorn. You have deeper contact with friends now. You find meaning through friends and groups. You work for the common good, but keep an eye on your own wishes and dreams.

Wednesday, May 14 (Moon in Scorpio There's a full moon in your eleventh house, which suggests that you reap what you've sown related to friend or a group of like-minded individuals. Your wishes and dreams are highlighted. With Saturn closely conjunct, you might be somewhat possessive of your ideas and ideals.

Thursday, May 15 (Moon into Sagittarius, 1:45 a.m.) It's a number 1 day, and that means you're at the top of your cycle. You get a fresh start, a new beginning. You can take the lead now, and don't be afraid to turn in a new direction. Stress originality in whatever you're doing.

Friday, May 16 (Moon in Sagittarius) The moon is in your twelfth house today. Think carefully before you act. A matter from the past could rise up again. Avoid any self-destructive behavior. Be aware of hidden enemies. It's a good day to work behind the scenes.

Saturday, May 17 (Moon into Capricorn, 4:13 a.m.) It's a number 3 day. You can influence people with your upbeat attitude today. Your charm and wit are appreciated. Your attitude determines everything. Spread your good news. Ease up on routines, and remain flexible.

Sunday, May 18 (Moon in Capricorn) The moon is on your ascendant today. Your face is in front of the public. Your appearance and personality shine. You're physically vital, and relations with the opposite sex go well. You're recharged for the month ahead, and this makes you more appealing to the public.

Monday, May 19 (Moon into Aquarius, 5:59 a.m.) With Mars going direct in your tenth house today, Capricorn, you tend to be quite aggressive in your career. You're pushing hard for an advancement, raise, or elevation in prestige. You feel best when coworkers are on the same path. You're looking to move ahead in a big way, and you're ready and willing to act.

Tuesday, May 20 (Moon in Aquarius)   The moon is in your second house today. It's a good day for finances and investments. Money and material goods are important to you and give you a sense of security. You feel best when surrounded by familiar objects, especially at home. It's not the objects themselves that are important, but the fond memories associated with them.

Wednesday, May 21 (Moon into Pisces, 8:19 a.m.) It's a mystery day, Capricorn. Secrets, intrigue, confidential information play a role. Be aware of decisions made behind closed doors. You work best on your own today. Knowledge is essential to success. Go with the flow. Express your desires, but avoid self-deception. Maintain your emotional balance.

Thursday, May 22 (Moon in Pisces)   The moon is in your third house today. Your mental abilities are strong, and you have an emotional need to reinvigorate your studies, especially regarding matters of the past. Alternately, past issues with siblings resurface. Speak you mind, tell others what you know, but stay in control of your emotions.

Friday, May 23 (Moon into Aries, 12:02 p.m.) It's a number 9 day. That means it's time to complete a project. Clear your desk, and make room for the new, but don't start anything until tomorrow. Spend some time in deep thought. Consider how you can expand your base.

Saturday, May 24 (Moon in Aries) The moon is in your fourth house today. Spend time with your family and other loved ones. Stick close to home. A parent could be involved in your day. You feel close to your roots now. See if you can remember a dream from last night.

Sunday, May 25 (Moon into Taurus, 5:28 p.m.) Cooperation is highlighted. You work well with others. Your intuition focuses on relationships, either a new one that's developing or a current one. Don't make waves. Don't rush or show resentment; let things develop. Show your appreciation to others.

Monday, May 26 (Moon in Taurus) The moon is in your fifth house today. It's a great day for pursuing a romance, Capricorn. There's greater emotional depth in whatever you pursue. Be yourself; be emotionally honest. You're creative and have the ability to tap deeply into the collective unconscious. Children and pets could play a role.

Tuesday, May 27 (Moon in Taurus)   Under the influence of the Taurus moon, your health and physical activity are highlighted. Go hiking; get out in nature. It's a good time for doing practical things, cultivating ideas. Try to avoid stubborn behavior when others question your actions. You could be somewhat possessive. While you maintain a common-sense, down-to-earth perspective on life, you also long for the good life with its material blessings.

Wednesday, May 28 (Moon into Gemini, 12:48 a.m.) Venus moves into your fifth house today. Relationships are harmonious and easygoing, especially with a romantic partner. You're feeling good about helping others. You receive good news about a creative project. Meanwhile, there's a new moon in your fifth house, and that suggests that new opportunities come your way related to that project. Whatever is coming will benefit you, especially if you keep control of your emotions. With Uranus forming a beneficial angle, positive changes affect you deeply.

Thursday, May 29 (Moon in Gemini)   Mercury moves into your seventh house today. You take a renewed interest in a partnership, either personal or business. A contract could be involved. You get your ideas across, and your intuition plays a role.

Friday, May 30 (Moon into Cancer, 10:14 a.m.) You work best on your own today. Secrets, intrigue, confidential information play a role. Be aware of decisions made behind closed doors. You investigate, analyze, or simply observe what's going on now. You quickly come to a conclusion and wonder why others don't see what you see. You detect deception and recognize insincerity with ease.

Saturday, May 31 (Moon in Cancer)   The moon is in your seventh house today. The focus turns to relationships, business and personal ones. You get along well with others. You can fit in just about anywhere. Loved ones and partners are more important than usual. A legal matter comes to your attention now. It could be a marriage.

JUNE 2014

Sunday, June 1 (Moon into Leo, 9:44 p.m.)   It's a number 6 day, a service day. Be understanding, and avoid confrontations. Diplomacy and compassion win the way. Focus on making people happy, but avoid scattering your energies. Be sympathetic, kind, and understanding.

Monday, June 2 (Moon in Leo)   With the moon in your eighth house, you take an interest in a spiritual or metaphysical subject. You dig deep for information about life after death, astrology, or past lives. You could become part of a group or movement dedicated to raising people's awareness.

Tuesday, June 3 (Moon in Leo)   Under the influence of the Leo moon, you're at center stage, Capricorn. Romance and love are highlighted, but maintain your emotional balance. Financial speculation could play a role, but that tends to go against your nature.

Focus on advertising and publicity. Dress boldly; showmanship is highlighted.

Wednesday, June 4 (Moon into Virgo, 10:21 a.m.) It's a number 9 day. Complete what you've been working on and get ready for something new. Consider ways to expand. Reflect on everything that has happened recently, and follow your intuitive nudges. Accept what comes your way. A new cycle is about to begin.

Thursday, June 5 (Moon in Virgo) The moon is in your ninth house today, the home of higher learning. Plan a trip or sign up for a seminar or workshop. A foreign country or person of foreign birth could play a role. Publicity and advertising are emphasized.

Friday, June 6 (Moon into Libra, 10:02 p.m.) It's a number 2 day. Use your intuition to get a sense of your day. Be kind and understanding. Cooperation, especially with partners, is highlighted. Don't make waves. Don't rush or show resentment; let things develop. Marriage or a partnership plays a key role.

Saturday, June 7 (Moon in Libra) Mercury goes retrograde in your seventh house today and stays there until July 1. What seemed crystal clear yesterday, especially regarding a partnership, turns somewhat foggy. Expect some confusion and disruption in relationships, personal and business, over the next three weeks. You could be facing delays related to communication with loved ones and partners, also computer glitches and travel delays. Keep in mind that it's temporary.

Sunday, June 8 (Moon in Libra)   The moon is in your tenth house today. Professional concerns take on more importance. You could get a promotion, raise, or pat on the back. You're more responsive to the needs and moods of a group and the public in general. You move up the ladder.

Monday, June 9 (Moon into Scorpio, 6:39 a.m.) Neptune turns retrograde in your third house today. You're getting intuitive nudges about problems with a sibling, other relative, or neighbor. But if you try to help, others might misunderstand your intentions, especially if they are out of the ordinary. Best to back off and avoid confusion.

Tuesday, June 10 (Moon in Scorpio)   With the moon in your eleventh house today, you gain through your business and personal contacts. Friends play an important role in your day. Focus on your wishes and dreams. Examine your overall goals. Those goals should be an expression of who you are.

Wednesday, June 11 (Moon into Sagittarius, 11:24 a.m.)   You work best on your own today. Secrets, intrigue, confidential information play a role. Be aware of decisions made behind closed doors. You investigate, analyze, or simply observe what's going on. You quickly come to a conclusion and wonder why others don't see what you see. You detect deception and recognize insincerity with ease.

Thursday, June 12 (Moon in Sagittarius)   The moon is in your twelfth house today. You might feel a need to withdraw and work on your own. Things concerning the past or your childhood play a role. You hide your emotions and moodiness. Take time to reflect and meditate.

Friday, June 13 (Moon into Capricorn, 1:05 p.m.) There's a full moon in your twelfth house today with Uranus forming a beneficial angle. That means you reap what you've sown related to a matter from the past. You're recharged for the remainder of the month. Something secret or hidden becomes clearer. Don't attract attention to what you know.

Saturday, June 14 (Moon in Capricorn) The moon is on your ascendant today. You're recharged for the rest of the month, and this makes you more appealing to the public. You're physically vital, and relations with the opposite sex go well. You're very good at keeping everyone around you in balance, Capricorn.

Sunday, June 15 (Moon into Aquarius, 1:28 p.m.) Use your intuition to get a sense of your day. Be kind and understanding. Cooperation, especially with partners, is highlighted. Don't make waves. Don't rush or show resentment; let things develop. Marriage plays a key role.

Monday, June 16 (Moon in Aquarius) The moon is in your second house today. That means that you can expect emotional experiences related to money. Money and material goods are important to you and give you a sense of security. Collect what's owed you, and pay what you owe. Watch your spending.

Tuesday, June 17 (Moon into Pisces, 2:26 p.m.)
It's a number 4 day. Your organizational skills are highlighted. Control your impulses. Persevere to get things done today, and don't get sloppy. Tear down the old in order to rebuild. Be methodical and thorough. Revise, rewrite.

Wednesday, June 18 (Moon in Pisces)   The moon is in your third house today. Your mental abilities are strong, and you have an emotional need to reinvigorate your studies, especially regarding matters of the past. Take what you know, and share it with others. Stay in control of your emotions, especially when dealing with siblings, other relatives, or neighbors.

Thursday, June 19 (Moon into Aries, 5:26 p.m.)
It's a number 6 day, a service day. A domestic adjustment works out for the best. You could face emotional outbursts by someone making unfair demands. Be understanding and diplomatic. Avoid confrontations or stubborn behavior, Capricorn. Help others, but dance to your own tune.

Friday, June 20 (Moon in Aries)   The moon is in your fourth house today. Spend time with your family and other loved ones. Stick close to home, if possible. It's a good day to retreat to a private place to meditate. You're dealing with the foundations of who you are and who you are becoming. A parent plays a role in your day.

Saturday, June 21 (Moon into Taurus, 11:03 p.m.)
It's a number 8 day, your power day and your day to

play it your way. You can go far with your plans and achieve financial success. Be aware that fear of failure or fear that you won't measure up will attract tangible experiences that reinforce the feeling.

Sunday, June 22 (Moon in Taurus)   The moon is in your fifth house today. You're in touch with your creative side, but your emotions tend to overpower your intellect. There's greater depth to a love relationship. You might be somewhat possessive of loved ones, particularly children.

Monday, June 23 (Moon in Taurus)   Venus moves into your sixth house today. Romance in the workplace is highlighted. Maybe it's a flirtation, but it could turn more serious. Alternately, the workplace is harmonious, and you enjoy being there. Artistic endeavors play a role.

Tuesday, June 24 (Moon into Gemini, 7:06 a.m.) The spotlight is on cooperation. New relationships could form. Your emotions and sensitivity are highlighted. There could be some soul searching related to older relationships. Flow with the current; accept what comes your way.

Wednesday, June 25 (Moon in Gemini)   With the moon in your sixth house today, the emphasis turns to your daily work and helping others. Attend to details, and be careful not to overlook any seemingly minor matters that could take on importance. Keep up with your exercise plan, and watch your diet.

Thursday, June 26 (Moon into Cancer, 5:06 p.m.)
It's a number 4 day, and that means the emphasis today is on your organizational skills. In romance your persistence pays off. You're building a foundation for the future. Control your impulses to wander off to another task; fulfill your obligations. You can overcome bureaucratic red tape.

Friday, June 27 (Moon in Cancer)   There's a new moon in your seventh house today. New opportunities appear related to a partnership. It could involve a legal matter. Women play a prominent role. Loved ones and partners are more important than usual. However, beware of possible conflict with a loved one.

Saturday, June 28 (Moon in Cancer)   The moon remains in your seventh house today. The focus turns to relationships, business and personal ones. You get along well with others. You can fit in just about anywhere. Loved ones and partners are more important than usual. A legal matter comes to your attention. It could be a marriage.

Sunday, June 29 (Moon into Leo, 4:44 a.m.)   It's a number 7 day. Secrets, intrigue, confidential information play a role. Be aware of decisions made behind closed doors. You work best on your own today. Knowledge is essential to success. Go with the flow. Express your desires, but avoid self-deception. Maintain your emotional balance.

Monday, June 30 (Moon in Leo)   With the moon in your eighth house, you take an interest in a spiritual or metaphysical subject. You dig deep for information about life after death, astrology, or past lives. You could become part of a group or movement dedicated to raising people's awareness.

JULY 2014

Tuesday, July 1 (Moon into Virgo, 5:25 p.m.) Mercury goes direct in your sixth house. Confusion, delays, and miscommunication are over related to your daily work and any health concerns. You handle mental work very well, especially dealing with computers and electronic devices. The glitches you've experienced are in the past. A matter related to your willingness or ability to help others becomes much more clear.

Wednesday, July 2 (Moon in Virgo) The moon is in your ninth house today. You're a dreamer and thinker. You can create positive change through your ideas. You guide others in their intellectual development. A foreign-born person or a foreign country plays a role in your day.

Thursday, July 3 (Moon in Virgo) Under the influence of the Virgo moon, you feel an urge to exercise and watch your diet. Take care of details, especially related to your health. Stop worrying and fretting. Take time to write in a journal. You write from a deep place with lots of details and colorful descriptions. Dig deep for info.

Friday, July 4 (Moon into Libra, 5:44 a.m.) It's a number 1 day, and that means you're at the top of your cycle again. You get a fresh start and attract creative people to your cause. Avoid naysayers, and don't be afraid to turn in a new direction. In romance a flirtation could turn serious. Happy Independence Day!

Saturday, July 5 (Moon in Libra)   The moon is in your tenth house today. Your life is more public. You gain an elevation in prestige. You're more responsive to the needs and moods of a group and the public in general. You work for the common good, but keep an eye on your own wishes and dreams.

Sunday, July 6 (Moon into Scorpio, 3:34 p.m.)   It's a number 3 day. Ease up on your routines. Your attitude determines everything today. Take time to relax, enjoy yourself, recharge your batteries. You can influence people with your upbeat attitude.

Monday, July 7 (Moon in Scorpio)   The moon is in your eleventh house today, Capricorn. Your friendships expand as new people come into your life. You find strength in numbers and meaning through friends and groups. Focus on your wishes and dreams. But take a close look at your responsibilities and obligations, and follow through on them. Make sure that you're not hurting anyone with whatever you're doing.

Tuesday, July 8 (Moon into Sagittarius, 9:25 p.m.)   You're restless and looking for change, a new perspective. You're versatile and changeable. Take risks, experiment, and pursue a new idea, but be careful not to overcommit yourself. Freedom of thought and action is key.

Wednesday, July 9 (Moon in Sagittarius)   The moon is in your twelfth house today. Think carefully before you act. There's a tendency now to undo all the positive actions you've taken. Avoid any self-destructive behavior. Be aware of hidden enemies. It's a good day to work behind the scenes.

Thursday, July 10 (Moon into Capricorn, 11:25 p.m.)   It's a number 7 day. You work best on your own today. Gather information, but don't make any absolute decisions until tomorrow. Go with the flow. Avoid confusion and conflicts. Keep any secrets entrusted to you.

Friday, July 11 (Moon in Capricorn)   With the moon in your first house today, you feel restless and uncertain. Your feelings fluctuate from moment to moment. It's a good time to revise your goals. You're responsive to others and also sensitive to their concerns. The people around you tend to influence your thoughts and actions more than usual.

Saturday, July 12 (Moon into Aquarius, 11:07 p.m.)   Mercury moves into your seventh house today. That means you get your ideas across about a partnership. Your mind is especially quick, and you make your point clearly. However, make sure your arguments with a partner are fully conceived. There's also a full moon in your first house, indicating that you reap what you've sown related to your personal life. Your health and outlook toward the public become clearer to you.

Sunday, July 13 (Moon in Aquarius)   The moon is in your second house today. Yesterday's energy flows into your Sunday. It's a great day for finances. Expect emotional experiences related to money. You equate your financial assets with emotional security. Look at your priorities in handling your income.

Monday, July 14 (Moon into Pisces, 10:41 p.m.) It's a number 2 day. It's all about partnerships, cooperation, working together to get things done. Look for a new relationship to develop. Use your intuition to get a sense of how it will work out. Help comes through friends.

Tuesday, July 15 (Moon in Pisces)   The moon is in your third house today. That means you communicate well but tend to get emotional, especially when dealing with siblings and other relatives, even neighbors. Matters from the past intrigue you now. Be careful if you're driving and talking on your cell. Eyes on the road; hands on the wheel.

Wednesday, July 16 (Moon in Pisces)   Jupiter moves into your eighth house today, where it stays for a year. Shared possessions are highlighted. An inheritance could figure in. You have an opportunity to expand whatever you're doing and move ahead. A partner plays an important role. Spiritual values arise.

Thursday, July 17 (Moon into Aries, 12:07 a.m.)
It's a number 5 day. That means you're open to change and variety, and you desire to loosen any restrictions today. You're willing to take a risk and experiment. Variety is the spice of life, and change is good. Think outside the box.

Friday, July 18 (Moon in Aries)   Venus moves into your seventh house today. A relationship is quite harmonious. Marriage or a partnership is important to you, and you contribute more than your share to the relationship. You get along well with others, especially with a partner. Everything looks quite prosperous!

Saturday, July 19 (Moon into Taurus, 4:43 a.m.)
Look beneath the surface for the reasons others are shifting their points of view, changing their tune. Be aware of decisions made behind closed doors. Secrets, intrigue, confidential information play a role.

Sunday, July 20 (Moon in Taurus)   Saturn goes direct in your eleventh house today. Over the coming months, friends and or members of group are on your mind, and you do your best to hide your emotions and moodiness. You could face delays related your pursuit of your wishes and dreams. Keep close tabs on your emotions, especially when dealing with institutions such as hospitals, courtrooms or government offices. You feel most comfortable in your home environment.

Monday, July 21 (Moon into Gemini, 12:37 p.m.)
Uranus goes retrograde in your fourth house, and that

could mean some erratic and unexpected developments related to your home life. Try to avoid making mountains out of molehills. You may be looking into selling your house and relocating or renovating your home. You could also experience bursts of intuitive energy that help you with your plans.

Tuesday, July 22 (Moon in Gemini)   With the moon in your sixth house today, the emphasis turns to your daily work and helping others. Attend to details, and be careful not to overlook any seemingly minor matters that could take on importance. Keep up with your exercise plan, and watch your diet.

Wednesday, July 23 (Moon into Cancer, 11:00 p.m.) It's a number 2 day. Cooperation is highlighted today. Use your intuition to get a sense of your day. Be kind and understanding. Show your appreciation to others. There could be some soul searching related to relationships.

Thursday, July 24 (Moon in Cancer)   With the moon in your seventh house, you get along well with others. You can fit in just about anywhere. Loved ones and partners are more important than usual. Women play a particularly prominent role today, and there could be a contract involved. Be careful that others don't manipulate your feelings.

Friday, July 25 (Moon in Cancer)   Mars moves into your eleventh house today. You put a lot of energy into a cause. You can excite people to support your goals, especially if you are working for the common good. You initiate action and are able to organize the masses. However, your strong sense of independence can make you your own worst enemy. Try not to disrupt the flow.

Saturday, July 26 (Moon into Leo, 10:56 a.m.) With the new moon in your eighth house, new opportunities come your way related to shared belongings. You communicate well with a partner. Security is an important issue with you right now. It can affect your feelings about your possessions, as well as things that you share with others, such as a spouse. With Jupiter favorably aligned, you see the big picture, Capricorn, and it works to your advantage.

Sunday, July 27 (Moon in Leo) The moon in your eighth house can affect your feelings about your possessions, as well as things that you share with others, such as a spouse. You have a strong sense of duty and feel obligated to fulfill your promises. Security is an important issue with you right now.

Monday, July 28 (Moon into Virgo, 11:37 p.m.) Secrets, intrigue, confidential information play a role today. You might feel best working on your own. You investigate, analyze, or simply observe what's going on. You quickly come to a conclusion and wonder why others don't see what you see. It's best to hold off on making any final decisions for a couple of days.

Tuesday, July 29 (Moon in Virgo) The moon is in your ninth house today. You're captivated by new ideas and philosophies. You're a dreamer and thinker.

You may feel a need to get away now, a break from the usual routine. You're feeling restless and yearn for a new experience.

Wednesday, July 30 (Moon in Virgo)   Under the influence of the Virgo moon, it's a good time to take care of details, especially related to a contract or partnership. Stop worrying and fretting. Dig deep for information. Take time to write in a journal. You write from a deep place with lots of details and colorful descriptions. Remember to exercise, and watch your diet.

Thursday, July 31 (Moon into Libra, 12:10 p.m.) It's a number 1 day, and you're at the top of your cycle again. Be independent and creative, and refuse to be discouraged by naysayers. Trust your hunches. Intuition is highlighted. You're inventive and make connections that others overlook. You're determined and courageous today. A flirtation could turn more serious.

AUGUST 2014

Friday, August 1 (Moon in Libra)   The moon is in your tenth house today. Professional concerns take on more importance. You could get a promotion, raise, or pat on the back. You're more responsive to the needs and moods of a group and the public in general. You move up the ladder.

Saturday, August 2 (Moon into Scorpio, 10:57 p.m.) It's a number 9 day. Finish what you've started, and get ready for the new. Clear up odds and ends. Visualize for the future. Set your goals, and make them so. But don't start anything new today.

Sunday, August 3 (Moon in Scorpio)   You're passionate, and your sexuality is heightened. You find strength in numbers and meaning through friends and groups. Social consciousness plays a role. You work for the common good, but keep an eye on your own wishes and dreams.

Monday, August 4 (Moon in Scorpio)   Under the influence of the Scorpio moon, yesterday's energy flows into your Monday. You're passionate about whomever or whatever you're focused on. Your emotions grow intense as you investigate an important matter. Control issues arise. Be aware of things happening in secret. Forgive and forget; try to avoid going to extremes.

Tuesday, August 5 (Moon into Sagittarius, 6:19 a.m.) You're warm and receptive to what others say. Your imagination is keen; you're curious and inventive. Enjoy the harmony, beauty, and pleasures of life. You have a strong sense of duty and feel obligated to fulfill your promises.

Wednesday, August 6 (Moon in Sagittarius)   The moon is in your twelfth house today. It's a good day to work behind the scenes and avoid any conflict. You could be dealing with a matter from the past that has returned to haunt you. Keep your feelings secret. Follow your intuition.

Thursday, August 7 (Moon into Capricorn, 9:39 a.m.)   It's a number 5 day. Freedom of thought and action is highlighted, as are change and variety. Think outside the box; think freedom. Promote new ideas; follow your curiosity. Look for adventure.

Friday, August 8 (Moon in Capricorn)   The moon is on your ascendant today. You're recharged for the month ahead, and this makes you more appealing to the public. It's a great day for starting something new. Your appearance and personality shine. Your feelings and thoughts are aligned. Dealings with the opposite sex go well.

Saturday, August 9 (Moon into Aquarius, 9:53 a.m.)   It's a number 7 day. Secrets, intrigue, confidential information play a role. Be aware of decisions made behind closed doors. Knowledge is essential to success. Go with the flow. Express your desires, but avoid self-deception. Maintain your emotional balance.

Sunday, August 10 (Moon in Aquarius)   There's a full moon in your second house today. You gain insight and illumination related to finances, neighbors, or your community. You reap what you've sown regarding a matter from the past. With Uranus forming a beneficial angle, you gain sudden insight related to your everyday life.

Monday, August 11 (Moon into Pisces, 8:56 a.m.)   Finish what you've started, and get ready for the new. Clear up odds and ends. Visualize for the future. Set your goals, and make them so. But don't start anything today. Strive for universal appeal.

Tuesday, August 12 (Moon in Pisces)   Venus moves into your eighth house today. You benefit from possessions you share with a partner. You also could take an interest in exploring reincarnation or life after death. Matters of sex, death, rebirth, rituals, and relationships could also play a role in your day. Alternately, you could be dealing with mortgages, insurance, investments, or an inheritance.

Wednesday, August 13 (Moon into Aries, 9:01 a.m.) Partnerships are highlighted. Use your intuition to get a sense of your day, and focus on relationships. Be kind and understanding. The spotlight is on cooperation. Emotions and your sensitivity play a role.

Thursday, August 14 (Moon in Aries)   The moon is in your fourth house today. You're dealing with the foundations of who you are. Take the day off, if possible, or work at home. Spend some time in meditation. It's a good day to handle repairs or beautify your home. Family and loved ones are important.

Friday, August 15 (Moon into Taurus, 11:59 a.m.) Mercury moves into your ninth house today, indicating an interest in philosophy, religion, law, or publishing. You communicate well, speaking your mind clearly and authoritatively. You express your ideas and opinions to whoever will listen. You could be discussing plans for a long journey. A foreign-born person might play an important role.

Saturday, August 16 (Moon in Taurus)   With the moon in your fifth house today, it's a good day to take a chance and speculate. Your emotions tend to overpower your intellect. You might be somewhat possessive of loved ones now, particularly children. You're also more involved with creative facets of your life. Be yourself; be emotionally honest. In love there's greater emotional depth to a relationship.

Sunday, August 17 (Moon into Gemini, 6:42 p.m.) It's a number 6 day, a service day. Diplomacy is called for. Be sympathetic and kind, generous and tolerant. Focus on making people happy. Do a good deed for someone, but dance to your own tune.

Monday, August 18 (Moon in Gemini)   The moon is in your sixth house today. It's a good day to exercise and watch your diet. Help others, maybe visiting someone who is sick, but don't fall into the trap of martyrdom. Attend to details related to your health. Make a doctor or dentist appointment. Your personal health occupies your attention now.

Tuesday, August 19 (Moon in Gemini)   Under the influence of the Gemini moon, you're mentally quick and communicate well. You see two sides of an issue. You're feeling creative and need to express yourself in writing. A change of scenery would do you good today, possibly a short trip to visit friends or relatives.

Wednesday, August 20 (Moon into Cancer, 4:46 a.m.)   It's a number 9 day. That means the old cycle is ending, and a new one is about to begin. Look for a new approach, a new perspective. You'll probably find that old ways have outlived their usefulness. Look beyond the immediate. Spiritual values surface.

Thursday, August 21 (Moon in Cancer) The moon is in your seventh house today. You get along well with others. A relationship plays an important role in your day. Loved ones and partners are more important than usual. But don't allow anyone to manipulate your feelings.

Friday, August 22 (Moon into Leo, 4:50 p.m.) It's a number 2 day. Use your intuition to get a sense of your day. Be kind and understanding. Cooperation, especially with partners, is highlighted. Don't make waves. Don't rush or show resentment; let things develop. Marriage or a partnership plays a key role.

Saturday, August 23 (Moon in Leo) With the moon in your eighth house, you could attract people with power to you today. Your energy is more intense than usual, and drama plays a role. Your emotions could affect your feelings about belongings that you share with others. An interest in metaphysics or related rituals grabs your attention.

Sunday, August 24 (Moon in Leo) Under the influence of the Leo moon, theatrics and drama are highlighted. You're at center stage today. You like to flaunt and celebrate. Be wild, imaginative; be the person you always imagined you might be. Play with different personae.

Monday, August 25 (Moon into Virgo, 5:33 a.m.)
There's a new moon in your ninth house. That could mean you get an opportunity for long-distance travel or continuing your education or both. A foreign-born person or a foreign country plays a role. Worldviews are emphasized.

Tuesday, August 26 (Moon in Virgo)   Yesterday's energy flows into your Tuesday. You're feeling as if you need to get away. You yearn for a new experience. Plan a long trip or sign up for a seminar or workshop. You're a dreamer and thinker. Look to the big picture.

Wednesday, August 27 (Moon into Libra, 5:54 p.m.)
It's your mystery day, Capricorn. You might feel best working on your own. You investigate, analyze, or simply observe what's going on. You quickly come to a conclusion and wonder why others don't see what you see. It's best to hold off on making any final decisions for a couple of days.

Thursday, August 28 (Moon in Libra)   The moon is in your tenth house today, and that means professional concerns take priority as the work week ends. After your positive day yesterday, you could gain favor from bosses or the public. It's a good day for sales and dealing with the public. You're more responsive to the needs of others, especially coworkers.

Friday, August 29 (Moon in Libra)   Under the influence of the Libra moon, romance is highlighted. Relationship issues figure prominently in your day.

It's a great day to schedule an adventurous encounter with your significant other. You're also looking for balance as you fine-tune a love relationship. Compassion is highlighted.

Saturday, August 30 (Moon into Scorpio, 4:53 a.m.)
It's a number 1 day, and that means you're at the top of your cycle. You get a fresh start, a new beginning. You can take the lead, and don't be afraid to turn in a new direction. Stress originality in whatever you're doing.

Sunday, August 31 (Moon in Scorpio)   The moon is in your eleventh house, Capricorn, the native home of your sign. You work well with others, especially in a group. Friends play a surprisingly important role, especially Taurus and Virgo. Focus on your wishes and dreams. Examine your overall goals, and make sure that they're still an expression of who you are.

SEPTEMBER 2014

Monday, September 1 (Moon into Sagittarius, 1:17 p.m.)   It's a number 9 day, a great time for completing projects and getting ready for something new. Clear up odds and ends. Take an inventory on where things are going in your life. Look beyond the present, but don't start anything until tomorrow.

Tuesday, September 2 (Moon in Sagittarius)
With Mercury moving into your tenth house today, you communicate well this month, especially related to your career and career goals. If you're looking for

a raise or promotion, go for it this month. You can convince bosses, and you get the support of colleagues.

Wednesday, September 3 (Moon into Capricorn, 6:16 p.m.) Partnerships are highlighted. Use your intuition to get a sense of your day, and focus on relationships. Be kind and understanding. The spotlight is on cooperation. Emotions and your sensitivity play a role.

Thursday, September 4 (Moon in Capricorn) With the moon on your ascendant today, Capricorn, you're recharged for the rest of the month, and this makes you more appealing to the public. The way you see yourself now is the way others see you. You're physically vital, and relations with the opposite sex go well. Your thoughts about self and health are key.

Friday, September 5 (Moon into Aquarius, 8:00 p.m.) Venus moves into your ninth house today. Your intuition is highlighted. You could be launching an extended pleasure trip, or at least planning one. Romance is in the air, and a foreign-born person or a foreign country could play a role. You enjoy studying philosophy and art, and you are open to people of different cultures and races.

Saturday, September 6 (Moon in Aquarius) The moon is in your second house today. Your ideals play an important role. Whatever you value takes on more importance. It's a good day to deal with finances and money issues. You feel best surrounded by your belongings. It's not the objects that are important, but the way they make you feel.

Sunday, September 7 (Moon into Pisces, 7:48 p.m.)
It's a number 6 day, and service to others is the theme. It's time to be diplomatic. Be sympathetic and kind, generous and tolerant. Focus on making people happy. Your life is more public today. You're more responsive to the needs and moods of a group.

Monday, September 8 (Moon in Pisces) There's a full moon in your third house today. You reap what you've sown related to your siblings, family, or neighbors. It's a good time to complete a project related to your community. Your mind is quick, and you get your ideas across. You gain insight into whatever mental activity you've been working on lately. With Saturn forming a beneficial angle, whatever you hear about is a serious matter. Saturn also brings more structure into your work life and allows you to take advantage of what you've learned.

Tuesday, September 9 (Moon into Aries, 7:34 p.m.)
It's a number 8 day, your power day. You have a chance to expand and gain recognition, even fame and power. You attract financial success. You're in the power seat, especially if you open your mind to a new approach that could bring in big bucks.

Wednesday, September 10 (Moon in Aries) The moon is in your fourth house today. Spend time with your family and other loved ones. Work on a project to beautify your home. It's a good day to stay close to home. Take time to meditate. Try to remember your dreams.

Thursday, September 11 (Moon into Taurus, 9:17 p.m.)   It's a number 1 day, so you're at the top of your cycle. Get out and meet new people, have new experiences, do something you've never done before. You're determined and courageous now. A flirtation turns more serious. Explore and discover. Creativity is highlighted.

Friday, September 12 (Moon in Taurus)   The moon is in your fifth house today. Your creativity is enhanced. You can dig deep for inspiration. Your emotions tend to overpower your intellect. You're strongly attached to loved ones, particularly children, but eventually you need to let go.

Saturday, September 13 (Moon in Taurus)   Mars moves into your twelfth house today. You have strong desires and might feel that you're on a mission. However, you tend to keep your thoughts secret and work behind the scenes. Any suppressed anger that you're feeling needs to be brought into the open.

Sunday, September 14 (Moon into Gemini, 2:27 a.m.)   It's a number 4 day. Emphasize quality in whatever you're doing. You're building a creative foundation for your future. Tear down the old in order to rebuild. Get organized; be methodical and thorough. Take care of your obligations.

Monday, September 15 (Moon in Gemini)   The moon is in your sixth house today. It's another service-oriented day. You improve, edit, and refine the work of others. Visit someone who is sick. It's a good day to clarify any health or work issues. It's best if you follow a regular schedule now.

Tuesday, September 16 (Moon into Cancer, 11:24 a.m.)   It's a number 6 day. Service to others is the theme of the day. Diplomacy wins the way. You offer advice and support. Be understanding, and avoid confrontations. A domestic adjustment works out for the best.

Wednesday, September 17 (Moon in Cancer)   The moon is in your seventh house today. Partners in business or your personal life play a major role in your day. You're open and friendly to others. You look for ways to expand a friendship or partnership. Material gain is likely related to a partnership.

Thursday, September 18 (Moon into Leo, 11:10 p.m.)   It's another power day, Capricorn, a good day to buy a lotto ticket. Unexpected money arrives. You can go far with your plans and achieve financial success. Business discussions go well. You're playing with power, so be careful not to hurt others.

Friday, September 19 (Moon in Leo)   The moon is in your eighth house today. You have a strong sense of duty and feel obligated to fulfill your promises. Security is an important issue with you right now. An interest in metaphysics plays a role in your day. You could be exploring past lives, life after death, or maybe astrology.

Saturday, September 20 (Moon in Leo)   Under the influence of the Leo moon, you're at center stage, where you strut your stuff! Romance and love are highlighted. Financial speculation and gambling play a role. Focus on advertising and publicity. Dress boldly; showmanship is highlighted.

Sunday, September 21 (Moon into Virgo, 11:54 a.m.) It's a number 2 day. Cooperation is highlighted. You work well with others. Your intuition focuses on relationships, either a new one that's developing or a current one. Don't make waves. Don't rush or show resentment; let things develop. Show your appreciation to others.

Monday, September 22 (Moon in Virgo)   Pluto goes direct in your first house today. You feel very attuned to your personal outlook. It's all about your emotional self. Your feelings and thoughts are aligned, and you'll stay with these feelings for years. You're dealing with the person you are becoming. Be aware of any health issues, and see if you can diffuse them before they get out of control.

Tuesday, September 23 (Moon in Virgo)   The moon is in your ninth house today, the home of higher learning. Plan a trip or sign up for a seminar or workshop. A foreign country or person of foreign birth could play a role. Publicity and advertising are emphasized.

Wednesday, September 24 (Moon into Libra, midnight)   There's a new moon in your tenth house today, and that means new opportunities come your way related to your career and coworkers. You have a better understanding of a matter related to your profession. With Mars forming a beneficial angle, you take the lead and aggressively move ahead with your plans to advance in your career.

Thursday, September 25 (Moon in Libra)   The moon is in your tenth house today. Your focus turns to professional matters, whether career or education. You could be dealing with an issue related to your reputation, and it works out for the better. You get a boost in prestige. You are received well by others, but avoid making an emotional display in public.

Friday, September 26 (Moon into Scorpio, 10:30 a.m.)   It's a number 7 day. You investigate, analyze, or simply observe what's going on now. You quickly come to a conclusion and wonder why others don't see what you see. You detect deception and recognize insincerity with ease. Gather information, but don't make any absolute decisions until tomorrow. Go with the flow.

Saturday, September 27 (Moon in Scorpio)   Mercury moves into your eleventh house today. You speak and write well, especially related to a group activity. Friends play an important role in your day. You get your ideas across, and you work well with the public. Pay attention to your wishes and dreams, and make sure they remain a reflection of who you are.

Sunday, September 28 (Moon into Sagittarius, 6:51 p.m.)   It's a number 9 day, a great time for finishing whatever you've been working on and getting ready for something new. Clear up odds and ends. Take an inventory on where things are going in your life. Look beyond the present, but don't start anything new until tomorrow.

Monday, September 29 (Moon in Sagittarius)   Venus moves into your tenth house today. You move ahead in your career through social contacts. You could benefit career-wise from a marriage or partnership. Your personality shines, and that helps you advance in your profession.

Tuesday, September 30 (Moon in Sagittarius)   The moon is in your twelfth house today. It's a good day to withdraw from the action and work behind the scenes. You could be feeling especially sensitive. Matters from the past surface. Take time to turn inward and evaluate where you've been and where you're going. Keep your feelings to yourself, unless confiding in a close friend.

OCTOBER 2014

Wednesday, October 1 (Moon into Capricorn, 12:42 a.m.)   It's a number 1 day, Capricorn. Get out and meet new people. You get a fresh start now, a new beginning. Be independent and creative, and refuse to be discouraged by naysayers. You can take the lead on a new project. You're determined and courageous.

Thursday, October 2 (Moon in Capricorn) With
the moon remaining in your first house today, it's all
about your health and emotional self: how you feel
and how you feel about yourself. Your feelings and
thoughts are aligned. You get recharged for the remainder of the month and beyond.

Friday, October 3 (Moon into Aquarius, 4:01 a.m.)
It's a number 3 day. Take time to relax, enjoy yourself,
recharge your batteries. You can influence people
with your upbeat attitude. Your charm and wit are appreciated. Foster generosity. In romance you're an ardent and loyal lover.

Saturday, October 4 (Moon in Aquarius) Mercury goes retrograde in your eleventh house, where it
will stay until October 25. Personal matters related to
friends and your work with a group could get confus-
ing or delayed. Expect some delays and glitches in
communication over the next three weeks. Don't take
anything for granted; check and recheck everything.
Make sure that you communicate clearly so that others understand you.

Sunday, October 5 (Moon into Pisces, 5:25 a.m.)
It's a number 5 day. Change and variety are highlighted. Think freedom, no restrictions. Release old
structures; get a new point of view. You're versatile
and changeable, but be careful not to spread out and
diversify too much.

Monday, October 6 (Moon in Pisces) The moon
is in your third house today. Your communications

with others are subjective. Take what you know, and share it with others, but control your emotions. That's especially true when dealing with siblings and other relatives or neighbors. Your thinking is unduly influenced by things of the past.

Tuesday, October 7 (Moon into Aries, 6:07 a.m.) It's a number 7 day, a mystery day. You launch a journey into the unknown, investigating a secret matter. Something hidden surfaces. It's best to wait a day before you take action. Keep what you know to yourself for now. Go with the flow.

Wednesday, October 8 (Moon in Aries) Sudden unexpected events occur affecting home life. You might move suddenly, or your home goes on the market. There could be a pregnancy in your family. It's also a great time to launch a cutting-edge home-based business.

Thursday, October 9 (Moon into Taurus, 7:44 a.m.) It's a number 9 day. Finish what you started. Visualize the future; set your goals, then make them so. Look beyond the immediate. Clear up odds and ends. Take an inventory on where things are going in your life. It's a good day to make a donation to a worthy cause.

Friday, October 10 (Moon in Taurus) With the moon in your fifth house today, your imagination is fertile. It's a great time to dive into a creative project. Likewise, there's greater emotional depth in a relationship. Children play an important role in your day.

Saturday, October 11 (Moon into Gemini, 11:51 a.m.)   It's a number 2 day for you, Capricorn, and that means cooperation is highlighted. Use your intuition to get a sense of your day. Be kind and nurturing. Show your appreciation to others. A new relationship could be developing.

Sunday, October 12 (Moon in Gemini)   The moon is in your sixth house today. Your personal health occupies your attention. Keep your resolutions about exercise, and watch your diet. Attend to details related to your making a doctor or dentist appointment. Help others, but don't deny your own needs.

Monday, October 13 (Moon into Cancer, 7:31 p.m.) It's a number 4 day. Persevere to get things done today. Take care of details, and don't get sloppy. Revise, rewrite. Be methodical and thorough, and control your impulses. Fulfill your obligations. You're building foundations for an outlet for your creativity. You tend to exhibit some perfectionist details.

Tuesday, October 14 (Moon in Cancer)   The moon is in your seventh house today. Loved ones and partners are more important than usual, Capricorn. A legal matter comes to your attention. Women play a prominent role. Pay attention to how the public relates to you. You feel a need to be accepted. You're looking for security, but you have a hard time going with the flow.

Wednesday, October 15 (Moon in Cancer)   Under the influence of the Cancer moon, you could feel moody today and overly sensitive. It might seem as if the world is out to get you. It's not. Take plenty of breaks from your work. That will help you clear your head and improve your focus when you return to work.

Thursday, October 16 *(Moon into Leo, 6:30 a.m.)*
It's a number 7 day, a mystery day. You launch a journey into the unknown, investigating a secret matter. Something hidden surfaces. It's best to wait a day before you take action. Keep what you know to yourself for now. Go with the flow.

Friday, October 17 *(Moon in Leo)* The moon is in your eighth house today. Security is an important issue with you right now. It's a good day to deal with mortgages, insurance, and investments. You could be dealing with a partner's resources. A mystery of the unknown, such as life after death, comes into play.

Saturday, October 18 *(Moon into Virgo, 7:09 p.m.)*
Finish what you started. Visualize the future; set your goals, then make them so. Look beyond the immediate. Clear up odds and ends. Take an inventory on where things are going in your life. It's a good day to make a donation to a worthy cause.

Sunday, October 19 *(Moon in Virgo)* The moon is in your ninth house today. It's a good time to look at the big picture. Break away from your usual routine, and look for a broader approach, new information, new ideas. A foreign-born person or a foreign country could play a role.

Monday, October 20 (Moon in Virgo)   Under the influence of the Virgo moon, you're dealing with the details. Others rely on you for assistance. You also could be focusing on a health issue. Watch your diet, and take time to exercise.

Tuesday, October 21 (Moon into Libra, 7:13 a.m.) It's a number 3 day. Your attitude determines everything today, Capricorn. Overall, the social energy of the day is warm and welcoming. You're curious and inventive; ideas bubble forth. Your imagination is keen. Your popularity is on the rise.

Wednesday, October 22 (Moon in Libra)   The moon is in your tenth house today. Your life is more public. You communicate well and are more responsive to the needs and moods of a group and the public in general. It's a good day for sales and dealing with the public. You get a boost in prestige.

Thursday, October 23 (Moon into Scorpio, 5:11 p.m.)   Venus moves into your eleventh house today, and there's also a new moon in the same house. That means you get along well with your friends and enjoy their company. But also new opportunities could result from your association with friends or a group. You have a chance now to fulfill your wishes and dreams.

Friday, October 24 (Moon in Scorpio)   The moon is in your eleventh house today. You have deeper contact with friends. You find strength in numbers. You join a group of like-minded individuals. Focus on your wishes and dreams. Examine your overall goals, and make sure that those goals are an expression of who you are.

Saturday, October 25 (Moon in Scorpio) Mercury moves into your tenth house today, joining Venus. You communicate well with others, especially coworkers, Capricorn. You can convince a boss that you deserve a raise or promotion, if you feel that you do.

Sunday, October 26 (Moon into Sagittarius, 12:41 a.m.) Mars moves into your first house today, Capricorn. Following up on yesterday's positive career energy, you are quite assertive, letting others know exactly what you think and how you feel. You're more outgoing and aggressive. Others see you as ambitious. You're at center stage, and you strut your stuff!

Monday, October 27 (Moon in Sagittarius) With the moon in your twelfth house today, you tend to withdraw from public view, Capricorn. Unconscious attitudes can be difficult. So can relations with women. Keep your feelings secret. Work behind the scenes, and follow your intuition.

Tuesday, October 28 (Moon into Capricorn, 6:04 a.m.) It's a number 1 day, and you're at the top of your cycle. Be independent and creative, and refuse to be discouraged by naysayers. Stress originality, and trust your hunches. You're determined and courageous today. In romance a flirtation turns more serious.

Wednesday, October 29 (Moon in Capricorn)   The moon is on your ascendant today. The way you see yourself now is the way others see you. Your appearance and personality shine. You're recharged for the month ahead, and this makes you more appealing to the public, Capricorn. You're physically vital, and relations with the opposite sex go well.

Thursday, October 30 (Moon into Aquarius, 9:52 a.m.)   It's a number 3 day. Your attitude determines everything today, Capricorn. You communicate well. You're curious and inventive; ideas bubble forth. Your imagination is keen now. Your popularity is on the rise.

Friday, October 31 (Moon in Aquarius)   The moon is in your second house today. You tend to equate your financial assets with emotional security. You feel best surrounded by your stuff in your home environment. It's not the objects themselves that are important, but the feelings and memories you associate with them. Put off making any major purchases.

NOVEMBER 2014

Saturday, November 1 (Moon in Pisces)   The moon is in your third house today, your native home, Capricorn. Be aware that your thinking might be unduly influenced by the past. Take what you know, and share it with others. However, keep conscious control of your emotions when communicating. You write from a deep place.

***Sunday, November 2—Daylight Saving Time Ends
(Moon in Pisces)***   Under the influence of the Pisces moon, your imagination is highlighted. It's also a time for deep healing. Watch for psychic events, synchronicities. Keep track of your dreams, including your daydreams. Ideas are ripe. You can tap deeply into the collective unconscious for inspiration.

Monday, November 3 (Moon into Aries, 1:54 p.m.)
No time to play today. Put romance on the back burner. Get organized. Tear down the old in order to rebuild. Be methodical and thorough. Control your impulses. Stay focused, and persevere to get things done.

Tuesday, November 4 (Moon in Aries)   With the moon in your fourth house, it's a good day to stick close to home and spend time with loved ones. Your home life and your roots are important. It's all about your foundations, the person you are, and the one you are becoming.

***Wednesday, November 5 (Moon into Taurus, 4:34
p.m.)***   It's a number 6 day, a service-oriented day. You offer advice and support to those around you. Do a good deed for someone. Be sympathetic and kind, generous and tolerant. Diplomacy wins the way.

Thursday, November 6 (Moon in Taurus)   There's a full moon in your fifth house. You gain insight related to a romance or creative project. You reap what you've sown. Children could play a role. With Mars and Pluto forming beneficial angles, you're in the driver's seat. In spite of power plays taking place around you, you see the way ahead.

Friday, November 7 (Moon into Gemini, 8:45 p.m.)
It's a number 8 day, a power day, and you're in the power seat. You're ambitious and goal oriented. Remain confident and convinced that material success is within reach, if not already here. You're playing with power, so be careful not to hurt others.

Saturday, November 8 (Moon in Gemini)   Mercury moves into your sixth house today, where it stays until November 27. You're conversing more than usual with others in the workplace. You use logic to argue your points, and your mind is quick. Others are learning from you, gaining new knowledge. But your thoughts are also turning to your health and diet. It's a good time to act on whatever issue is involved.

Sunday, November 9 (Moon in Gemini)   The moon is in your sixth house today, another service day. You're the one others go to for help. Do what you can, but don't deny your own needs. Attend to details related to your health, Capricorn. Make a doctor or dentist appointment.

Monday, November 10 (Moon into Cancer, 3:39 a.m.)   It's a number 2 day, and that means a partnership. Your spouse or partner is at your side. Don't make waves or show resentment, but take time again today to consider the direction you're headed and your motivation for continuing on this path. Your intuition focuses on relationships.

Tuesday, November 11 (Moon in Cancer)   With the moon in your seventh house, you get along well with others. You can fit in just about anywhere. Loved ones and partners are more important than usual. Take time to consider how others see you. You're in the public eye.

Wednesday, November 12 (Moon into Leo, 1:45 p.m.)   Your organizational skills are highlighted, but try not to wander off task. Emphasize quality; you're building a creative foundation for your future. Tear down the old in order to rebuild. Be methodical and thorough.

Thursday, November 13 (Moon in Leo)   The moon is in your eighth house today. Things could get emotionally intense in your dealings with someone from the opposite sex. That's particularly true if you're facing issues related to shared belongings. You're sensitive and intuitive, and you could take an interest in a metaphysical topic, such as past lives.

Friday, November 14 (Moon in Leo)   You're at center stage today. You like to flaunt and celebrate. Be wild, imaginative; be the person you always imagined you might be. Play with different personae. Theatrics and drama are highlighted.

Saturday, November 15 (Moon into Virgo, 2:09 a.m.)   Neptune goes direct in your third house today. You can make good connections now with your spiritual beliefs and imagination. However, there could be some confusion and blurring of the boundaries between your ego and others'.

Sunday, November 16 (Moon in Virgo)   Venus moves into your twelfth house today and stays there until December 11. You enjoy spending time on your own, working behind the scenes, away from the daily chaos. You keep your thoughts and emotions to yourself and tend to be somewhat secretive. Alternately, you feel quite favorable about a matter related to an institution—a hospital, the courts, or a government office.

Monday, November 17 (Moon into Libra, 2:31 p.m.)   It's a number 9 day. Finish what you started. Visualize the future; set your goals, then make them so. Look beyond the immediate. Get ready for something new. Strive for universal appeal.

Tuesday, November 18 (Moon in Libra)   With the moon in your tenth house today, you're more responsive to the needs and moods of coworkers and the public in general. You're feeling ambitious, pushing ahead in your career. You've got your eye on a promotion. Aim high, shoot for the moon, no pun intended!

Wednesday, November 19 (Moon in Libra)   Under the influence of the Libra moon, you work to keep everyone in balance around you. Romance is highlighted; so are the creative arts. This is a great day to schedule an adventurous encounter with your significant other. Your friend is apt to be feeling as excited and enthusiastic about the day as you are.

Thursday, November 20 (Moon into Scorpio, 12:32 a.m.)   It's a number 3 day. You're creative and express yourself well today. Your artistic talents are highlighted. You're also warm and receptive to what others say. Your attitude determines everything. Ease up on routines, and take time to listen.

Friday, November 21 (Moon in Scorpio) The moon is in your eleventh house today. You have deeper contact with friends. You find strength in numbers. You join a group of like-minded individuals. Focus on your wishes and dreams. Examine your overall goals, and make sure that those goals are an expression of who you are.

Saturday, November 22 (Moon into Sagittarius, 7:20 a.m.) There's a new moon in your twelfth house today. By stepping away from the action and working behind the scenes you get a chance to start over, a new beginning, a new opportunity. You might also gain an opportunity through contact with a large institution, such as a hospital, government office, or corporation. It's a good time for any kind of therapy or inner work.

Sunday, November 23 (Moon in Sagittarius) The moon is in your twelfth house today. Unconscious attitudes can be difficult. You tend to keep your feelings secret. Relations with women can be difficult. Take time to pursue a mystical or spiritual discipline. Your intuition is heightened.

Monday, November 24 (Moon into Capricorn, 11:32 a.m.) Finish what you started. Visualize the future; set your goals, then make them so. Look beyond the immediate. Get ready for something new. Strive for universal appeal.

Tuesday, November 25 (Moon in Capricorn)　The moon is in your first house today. You're sensitive to other people's feelings. You may feel moody, withdrawn one moment, happy the next, then sad. It's all about your emotional self. Your feelings and thoughts are aligned. You're dealing with the person you are becoming.

Wednesday, November 26 (Moon into Aquarius, 2:23 p.m.)　Complete a project. Clear up odds and ends. Take an inventory on where things are going in your life. Visualize the future; set your goals, then make them so. Accept what comes your way now. It's all part of a cycle.

Thursday, November 27 (Moon in Aquarius)　Mercury moves into your twelfth house today. Any decisions you make are probably based on feelings rather than logic. Matters from the past affect your thinking. You tend to keep your thoughts to yourself on such matters.

Friday, November 28 (Moon into Pisces, 5:04 p.m.) It's a number 2 day. Cooperation is highlighted. Your intuition focuses on relationships. Don't make waves now. Just let things develop. Show your appreciation to others. Help comes through friends or loved ones, especially a partner.

Saturday, November 29 (Moon in Pisces)　The moon is in your third house today. Trust your hunches.

Express yourself dynamically, but control your emotions, especially in discussions with female relatives, siblings, and neighbors. Take what you know, and share it with others, especially those with creative minds.

Sunday, November 30 (Moon into Aries, 8:15 p.m.) It's a number 4 day and time to get focused. Persevere to get things done today, and don't get sloppy. Tear down the old in order to rebuild. Be methodical and thorough, and stay on task. Revise and rewrite.

DECEMBER 2014

Monday, December 1 (Moon in Aries)   With the moon in your fourth house, it's a good day to stick close to home, if that's an option. You're dealing with the foundations of who you are and who you are becoming. You feel a close tie to your roots. You could be dealing with parents. Take time to find a private place to meditate. It's a good day to recall your dreams from last night.

Tuesday, December 2 (Moon in Aries)   Under the influence of the Aries moon, it's a great time for initiating projects, launching new ideas, or just brainstorming. You're extremely persuasive, especially if you're passionate about what you're doing, selling, or trying to convey. However, there's a tendency toward recklessness, which could lead to an accident.

Wednesday, December 3 (Moon into Taurus, 12:16 a.m.)   It's a number 5 day. Change and variety are highlighted. Think freedom, no restrictions. Release old structures; get a new point of view. You're versatile and changeable, but be careful not to spread out and diversify too much.

Thursday, December 4 (Moon in Taurus)   Mars moves into your second house today and stays that way until January 12. Now you're energized to carry out your plans, especially related to finances. You're also aggressive in promoting your values to others. But be careful not to act in a way that would offend them.

Friday, December 5 (Moon into Gemini, 5:29 a.m.) It's a number 7 day, another mystery day. Discuss and defend your beliefs. But make sure you see things as they are, not as you wish them to be. Knowledge is essential to success. Spirituality is emphasized. Keep any secrets entrusted to you to yourself.

Saturday, December 6 (Moon in Gemini)   The full moon is in your sixth house today. Now you can reap what you've sown related to your daily work and service to others. With Uranus and Jupiter forming beneficial angles, you can expand what you're doing that involves providing a service. Positive changes in your work life come fast, as if out of nowhere.

Sunday, December 7 (Moon into Cancer, 12:35 p.m.) It's a number 9 day. So finish what you started. Clear up odds and ends. Make room for something new, but don't start anything new until tomorrow. Look beyond the immediate. Take an inventory on where things are going in your life.

Monday, December 8 (Moon in Cancer)   Jupiter goes retrograde in your eighth house today and stays that way until April 8. You could face some delays and misunderstandings related to shared possessions or finances. Try to keep control of your emotions when dealing with matters such as taxes, insurance, or an inheritance. Alternately, others might misunderstand your interest in expanding your pursuit of a meta-physical subject, such as life after death.

Tuesday, December 9 (Moon into Leo, 10:15 p.m.) It's a number 2 day. That means partnerships and co-operation are highlighted. Help comes through friends or loved ones, especially a partner. Don't make waves. Don't rush or show resentment; let things de-velop. You could be undergoing some soul searching related to a relationship.

Wednesday, December 10 (Moon in Leo)   Venus moves into your first house today, where it stays until January 1. Your self-awareness and appearance are important. You're dealing with your emotional self, and you feel great affection for the person you are becoming. You're physically vital, and relations with the opposite sex go very well. You're also more ap-pealing to the public.

Thursday, December 11 (Moon in Leo)   With the moon in your eighth house, Capricorn, you could at-tract powerful people to you today. Your energy is more intense than usual, and drama plays a role. Your emotions could affect your feelings about belongings that you share with others. An interest in metaphysics or related rituals grabs your attention.

Friday, December 12 (Moon into Virgo, 10:20 a.m.)
It's a number 5 day. Approach the day with an unconventional mindset. Let go of old ways of looking at things; get a new point of view. Variety is the spice of life. You're versatile and changeable, but don't spread yourself too thin.

Saturday, December 13 (Moon in Virgo) The moon is in your ninth house today. You're a dreamer and thinker. You're captivated by new ideas and philosophies. You may feel a need to get away now, a break from the usual routine. You're feeling restless and yearn for something new.

Sunday, December 14 (Moon into Libra, 11:05 p.m.)
It's a number 7 day. Secrets, intrigue, confidential information play a role today. You investigate, analyze, or simply observe what's going on now. You quickly come to a conclusion and wonder why others don't see what you see. You detect deception and recognize insincerity with ease.

Monday, December 15 (Moon in Libra) With the moon in your tenth house today, professional concerns are the focus of the day. You gain an elevation in prestige, possibly an advancement in your career. You're more responsive to the needs and moods of a group and the public in general.

Tuesday, December 16 (Moon in Libra) Mercury moves into your first house today, where it stays until January 5. You tend to search for ways to improve yourself. You communicate your ideas well about your emotions and health. You focus on how the public relates to you, and you get your ideas across. It's difficult to remain detached and objective.

Wednesday, December 17 (Moon into Scorpio, 9:52 a.m.) It's a number 1 day, and you're at the top of your cycle. It's your day to take the lead on a new project. Ignore the naysayers; trust your hunches. You attract creative people. You're determined and courageous. Stress originality.

Thursday, December 18 (Moon in Scorpio) The moon is in your eleventh house today. You find strength in numbers and meaning through friends and groups. Work for the common good, but keep an eye on your own wishes and dreams.

Friday, December 19 (Moon into Sagittarius, 4:56 p.m.) It's a number 3 day. You can influence people now with your upbeat attitude today. Your charm and wit are appreciated. Your attitude determines everything. Spread your good news. Ease up on routines, and remain flexible.

Saturday, December 20 (Moon in Sagittarius) The moon is in your twelfth house today. Think carefully before you act. There's a tendency now to undo all the positive actions you've taken. Avoid any self-destructive behavior. Be aware of hidden enemies. It's a good day to work behind the scenes.

Sunday, December 21 (Moon into Capricorn, 8:26 p.m.)   There's a new moon in your first house today. That means new opportunities come your way related to your personal life. It's a good time to get rid of a bad habit, such as smoking. You get a new outlook on your health picture. Meanwhile, with Uranus going direct in your fourth house, you could experience a sudden shift in fortune related to a domestic matter. You could suddenly sell your house or purchase a new one.

Monday, December 22 (Moon in Capricorn)   With the moon on your ascendant, you're in front of the public. Your appearance and personality shine. You're recharged for the month ahead, and this makes you more appealing to the public. You're physically vital, and relations with the opposite sex go well.

Tuesday, December 23 (Moon into Aquarius, 9:53 p.m.)   Saturn enters your twelfth house today, where it stays for two and a half years. That means issues could arise over coming months related to your past or secrets. It's best to fly beneath the radar. Don't attract attention to your plans until they are fully conceived. You also could be reevaluating your ideals or whatever you value. Keep close tabs on your emotions, especially when talking about issues related to institutions such as hospitals, courts, or corporate offices.

Wednesday, December 24 (Moon in Aquarius)
The moon is in your second house today. You think quickly, especially related to finances. You can come up with moneymaking ideas. You're very focused, and it's all about finances and your values. These are more oriented to material gain than the intellect.

Thursday, December 25 (Moon into Pisces, 11:08 p.m.)   It's a number 9 day. Finish what you started. Visualize the future; set your goals, then make them so. Look beyond the immediate. Get ready for something new. Strive for universal appeal. Merry Christmas!

Friday, December 26 (Moon in Pisces)   The moon is in your third house today. You have an emotional need to pursue your studies of subjects that interest you. Your intellectual curiosity requires continued nurturing and growth. Meanwhile, you're dealing with the everyday world. Expect a lot of running around, short trips here and there. Accept an invitation.

Saturday, December 27 (Moon in Pisces)   Under the influence of the Pisces moon, your imagination is highlighted. You respond emotionally to whatever is happening. Keep track of your dreams, including your daydreams. You can tap deeply into the collective unconscious for inspiration. It's a day for deep healing.

Sunday, December 28 (Moon into Aries, 1:36 a.m.)
It's a number 3 day. You're innovative and creative and communicate well now. Your charm and wit are appreciated. Your attitude determines everything to-

day. Remain flexible and open to sudden opportunity. In romance you're an ardent and loyal lover.

Monday, December 29 (Moon in Aries) The moon is in your fourth house today, and that means it's a good time to stick close to home and take care of domestic matters. It's a good day to work on a home-repair project. A parent could play a role in your day. You're feeling close to your roots.

Tuesday, December 30 (Moon into Taurus, 5:57 a.m.) Variety is the spice of life. Think outside the box. Take risks, experiment. Let go of old structures; get a new point of view. You're versatile and change-able, but be careful not to spread out and diversify too much.

Wednesday, December 31 (Moon in Taurus) The moon is in your fifth house today. Your creativity is enhanced. You can dig deep for inspiration. Your emotions tend to overpower your intellect. You're strongly attached to loved ones, particularly children, but eventually you need to let go.

HAPPY NEW YEAR!

SYDNEY OMARR

Born on August 5, 1926, in Philadelphia, Pennsylvania, **Sydney Omarr** was the only person ever given full-time duty in the U.S. Army as an astrologer. He is regarded as the most erudite astrologer of the twentieth century and the best known, through his syndicated column and his radio and television programs (he was Merv Griffin's "resident astrologer"). Omarr has been called the most "knowledgeable astrologer since Evangeline Adams." His forecasts of Nixon's downfall, the end of World War II in mid-term and his death in office ... these and many others are on the record and quoted enough to e considered "legendary."

ABOUT THE SERIES

This is one of a series of twelve *Sydney Omarr®
Day-by-Day Astrological Guides* for the signs of
2014. For questions and comments about the
book, go to www.sydneyomarr.blogspot.com.

Penguin Group (USA) Online

What will you be reading tomorrow?

Tom Clancy, Patricia Cornwell, W.E.B. Griffin,
Nora Roberts, William Gibson, Catherine Coulter,
Stephen King, Dean Koontz, Ken Follett, Nick Hornby,
Khaled Hosseini, Kathryn Stockett, Clive Cussler,
John Sandford, Terry McMillan, Sue Monk Kidd,
Amy Tan, J. R. Ward, Laurell K. Hamilton,
Charlaine Harris, Christine Feehan...

You'll find them all at
penguin.com
facebook.com/PenguinGroupUSA
twitter.com/PenguinUSA

*Read excerpts and newsletters, find tour schedules
and reading group guides, and enter contests.*

Subscribe to Penguin Group (USA) newsletters
and get an exclusive inside look
at exciting new titles and the authors you love
long before everyone else does.

PENGUIN GROUP (USA)
us.penguingroup.com

S0151